The
ANOVA
SOUS-VIDE
Precision Cooker Cookbook

101 DELICIOUS RECIPES WITH INSTRUCTIONS FOR PERFECT LOW-TEMPERATURE IMMERSION CIRCULATOR CUISINE!

BY

ISABELLE DAUPHIN

HHF PRESS
SAN FRANCISCO

Legal Notice

The information contained in this book is for entertainment purposes only. The content represents the opinion of the author and is based on the author's personal experience and observations. The author does not assume any liability whatsoever for the use of or inability to use any or all information contained in this book, and accepts no responsibility for any loss or damages of any kind that may be incurred by the reader as a result of actions arising from the use of information in this book. Use this information at your own risk.

The author reserves the right to make any changes he or she deems necessary to future versions of the publication to ensure its accuracy.

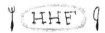

ISBN-13: 978-1537582146
ISBN-10: 1537582143-

Published in the United States of America
by Healthy Happy Foodie Press.

www.HHFpress.com

DO YOU LIKE FREE BOOKS?

Every month we release a new book, and we offer it to our current readers first...absolutely free! This helps us get early feedback before launching a book, and lets you stock your shelf full of interesting and valuable books for free!

Some recent titles include:

- The Complete Vegetable Spiralizer Cookbook
- My Lodge Cast Iron Skillet Cookbook
- 101 The New Crepes Cookbook

To receive this month's free book, just go to

http://www.healthyhappyfoodie.org/r2-freebooks

Table Of Contents

1

Why You Need This Book!

It's The ONLY Book Written Specifically for The Anova Immersion Circulator

You may have seen other books out there about sous vide cooking, but this is the only book that is written specifically to make you a sous vide expert using your Anova Immersion circulator. As you may already know, the Anova is the perfect tool for at home sous vide excellence and this book will offer pro tips and recipes to get the most out of your Anova. But that's not all. We're also going to discuss the science behind why the Anova is the single best option for at home sous vide cooking. You're going to learn how to put your Anova to work to make everything from breakfast to dessert using the safest and most reliable cooking method ever invented.

Get More Out of Your Anova Immersion Circulator

If you've already purchased the Anova Immersion Circulator you are probably interested in the science of sous vide. Many years ago, professional chefs running high volume kitchens ran into a problem: How to quickly serve food to a restaurant full of customers quickly and cooked properly. They stumbled upon an amazing idea: Cook food to the perfect temperature and then finish on the grill or under a broiler as needed. Suddenly high volume kitchens could finally keep up with the busy pace of a large restaurant. But they discovered that they could also cook nearly anything using this method. It took a while to catch on, but home cooks are now realizing that this method that has long kept busy restaurants running smoothly can be used at home to make meals easily and cooked to perfection. In this book we're going to show you that sous vide isn't just for the pros and it isn't just for making the perfect steak. We're going to unlock the true power of your Anova Immersion Circulator.

"Street-Wise" Pro Tips for Amazing Sous Vide Meals

Finally, the secrets of pro chefs are available to home chefs and we're going to explain all the ins and outs of how to make the most amazing meals using your Anova to cook sous vide. Our industry-tested tips will turn you into an expert in no time. We'll cover everything from how to get the best seal, to how you can use precise time and temperature using your Anova to create dishes you could have only dreamed about. Want fall off the bone barbecue ribs but you don't have a room for a smoker? Not a problem if you follow our exclusive tips to get the most out of your sous vide experience.

Over 100 Delicious Sous Vide Recipes!

Not only will this book teach you the techniques behind using the Anova to get the best sous vide results, it will also provide over one hundred recipes that will teach you how to make amazing vegetable, chicken, fish, pork, beef, lamb, and desserts, all using the sous vide method. In addition to the recipes, you will also learn the secrets behind some legendary rubs and seasonings that will make your dishes really come alive.

How to Use Your Anova Immersion Circulator

One of the main advantages of sous vide cooking is that you can start cooking and not have to keep checking on your food the whole time. Unlike commercial sous vide units, the Anova is meant for easy home use. In fact, all you need other t han the Anova is a container to hold enough water to submerge your food, and a device to vacuum seal the food for cooking. For sealing we recommend the Foodsaver. To operate your Anova, simply use the clamp screw to attach the unit to the side of a container, and pour enough water into the container to adequately cover the food. The Anova has a maximum fill line to let you know where to stop filling. Plug in the Anova, and using the temperature wheel on the display screen, set the temperature you want. Press the set button and the Anova will begin circulating and heating the water. To change to a different temperature, simply use the wheel to change temperatures and press set again. It really is that easy.

It's The ONLY Sous Vide Cookbook You Will Ever Need

Not only does this book offer amazing recipes and the science behind sous vide cooking, it will give you everything you need, from the preparation to the actual cooking, to make amazing sous vide dishes that will save time and energy. Best of all, your dishes will come out perfectly every time. This is why top chefs all over the world have been using sous vide cooking for decades. The Anova is the industry leading immersion circulator for some very good reasons. It is inexpensive, easy to used, and 100% accurate. Considering how easy the Anova is to use, it's no wonder that sous vide cooking is only becoming more popular with home cooks. Never again worry about over or undercooking your food. The Anova ensures that no matter what you are cooking, it will be perfect every time.

2

Why Use The Anova
for Sous Vide

It's All About Even Temperature

No matter what you're cooking, whether it's fish, a beautifully marbled steak, or delicate desserts, getting great results is all about controlling the temperature, and a couple of degrees absolutely will make all the difference. The Anova functions by circulating the cooking water and heating it to a very precise temperature. Because of this, everything you cook will be raised to this exact temperature and not a degree more or less. There is, literally, no cooking method on Earth that offers this level of precision, which is why professional chefs the world over rely on sous vide cooking to maintain the highest standards of cuisine.

Plan Meals Ahead of Time and Freeze Them

With the busy pace of life these days, preparing delicious home cooked meals every day can be a challenge. But with a vacuum sealer, you can prepare complete meals that can be frozen for months. Simply add all of your ingredients to the bag, seal it, pop it in the freezer, and then cook it the sous vide way using the Anova whenever you're ready. Because of the even heat that Anova offers, it cooks food much more evenly than a microwave. And because it uses much lower temperatures than a conventional oven, you can cook safely without supervision. When you pair your Anova immersion circulator with a vacuum-sealer, you can cook almost anything easily and quickly, with delicious results every time.

Sous Vide Locks In the Flavor.

Sous vide is French for "under vacuum" and it is this vacuum seal that creates two big advantages: First, it means that your food gets cooked evenly without any air inside the bag to create temperature problems. It also means that spices or marinades have constant contact with whatever you are cooking. This really presses the flavors directly into the food for extra tasty dishes.

The Anova Provides the Most Reliable Method for Perfectly Cooked Meals

Let's face it, most of us aren't professional chefs. But that doesn't mean we don't want to make a wide variety of excellent food. Cooking can be a challenge, and one of the most difficult aspects is knowing how hot you need to cook, and for how long. Luckily, the Anova Immersion Circulator is designed to take all of the guess work out of preparing your favorite meals. By strictly controlling the temperature, you can guarantee perfect results without years of practice. And with a high-quality vacuum sealer on hand, you know that your meals are cooking evenly.

It's Perfect for Those with Busy Schedules

Most of us can't afford to spend our whole day standing at the stove. And after a long day, no one looks forward to spending the rest of the evening in the kitchen making dinner. Well, thanks to the Anova, you don't have to. Many items like steaks and fish can be cook sous vide in less than an hour. So all you have to do is seal your food in a bag, set the Anova to the proper temperature, drop it in the water bath, and relax. There's no need to check up on your food. The Anova will do all the work for you. But let's say you feel like some barbecue pulled pork for dinner. Well, just set your Anova and pop it in the water bath in the morning and let it cook all day. The Anova is perfectly safe to use without supervision so you can make those delicious time consuming meals while you get on with the rest of your day.

It's The Healthiest and Safest Cooking Method

Since there is no direct contact with a heat source, you can avoid a lot of the excess fat and oil that is used in conventional cooking. This means that you can make healthier meals more often. But that's not the only health benefit of sous vide cooking. Because you aren't using high heat, there isn't the risk of losing nutrients that are destroyed at higher temperatures. Sous vide is also the safest cooking method because there are no high heat sources. The Anova is designed to run for extremely long periods of time with no supervision needed, so you can feel absolutely safe cooking while you're not home, or overnight.

3

The Surprising Health Benefits of Sous Vide Cooking

Preserve Those Nutrients!

Everyone is concerned about getting proper nutrition, but what you may not know is that certain cooking methods can actually destroy some of the vital nutrients that we need. Many types of food, including meats and vegetables can lose a great deal of their nutrients while being cooked over high heat. Some fat based nutrients can simply break down and become less beneficial, while others are lost as the juices cook out of the food. With sous vide cooking, however, you don't have to worry about losing those precious nutrients. Because sous vide uses much lower temperatures, the nutrients remain intact. And since the juices are all contained within the vacuum sealed bag, they don't have anywhere to go.

No Additional Oil Needed

Using traditional cooking methods, it's nearly impossible to cook without the use of fat. And while certain oils, such as olive oil, do have health benefits, others, like butter, are just adding unnecessary fat to your diet. Since food cooked with the sous vide method doesn't touch a hot surface, no oil is required in the cooking process. And since studies have shown that oils heated to high temperature can cause a variety of health issues, sous vide cooking completely eliminates this concern.

Plan Healthy Meals in Advance

Eating healthy every day can be a challenge mainly because of the time involved to prepare food. Sometimes it just feels easier to order a pizza or stop by the fast food place on the way home. But what if you could stock your freezer with healthy meals that you could prepare at a moment's notice? By spending some time to prepare healthy meals in advance and then vacuum sealing the raw ingredients, you can have months worth of healthy options ready to go. Considering how easy sous vide cooking is using the Anova, you really don't have any excuse not to eat healthy.

Using The Anova to Sous Vide Ensures Food Safety

It might seem strange to cook food at such a low temperature, but the idea behind sous vide cooking is to bring the food only to the exact desired temperature in order to prevent over or under cooking. This is why sous-vide has caught on so well with both professional chefs as well as home cooks. With no guess work, and no need to consult a thermometer, you can be assured that your food will come out cooked perfectly, but you can also rest assured that it is cooked to a safe temperature. This, combined with the fact that the food is vacuum sealed and not in danger of being contaminated by common kitchen bacteria, insures a safe and reliable cooking experience.

Only Use Plastic that is Safe to Cook With

You've probably heard about the dangers of food coming into contact with certain plastics, and the chemicals that can make their way into your food. Well, the good news is that Foodsaver's vacuum seal bags are designed specifically to be exposed to both heat and cold without any health risks commonly associated with plastic. Foodsaver bags are BPA free and microwave safe so you can have total peace of mind when using them to freeze, sous vide, or just reheat in the microwave.

4

How to Cook Anything Sous Vide

The Science of Sous Vide

Sous vide is French for "under vacuum" and has become increasingly popular for two reasons: It is incredibly reliable, and it produces tender, perfectly cooked food without the hassle of conventional cooking methods. With sous vide there is no guess work about whether your food is being cooked to the proper temperature, and no worries that it might be over or underdone. Food is sealed in a vacuum tight bag and submerged in a bath of water that is circulated and kept at the proper cooking temperature using a sous vide immersion circulator.

Sous Vide Equipment

It's true that sous vide cooking requires some additional equipment, but the great thing about sous vide is that you can use the exact same equipment to cook everything. As the term sous vide suggests, the most important part of the process is a good vacuum seal. Other than this, you will need the Anova immersion circulator to heat your water bath, and a container large enough to submerge whatever you want to cook.

What is a Sous Vide Immersion Circulator?

Excellent question! There are quite a few sous-vide units available these days and many of them are great for home use. Depending on the amount of food you're planning to cook, you can decide on how powerful a sous vide unit you will require. The Anova Immersion Circulator is inexpensive and does an excellent job cooking for up to eight people at a time. Simply attach the sous vide unit to the side of a container that can hold enough water to properly submerge your food (about 12 quarts), and set it to the desired temperature. The sous vide unit will let you know when it has reached that temperature, and then it's just a matter of putting your vacuum sealed food in the water and waiting.

5

How the Anova Immersion Circulator Works

Your Anova Immersion Circulator really couldn't be easier to use.

- You will notice that there is a clamp on the unit that can be fit to many types of containers. Simply mount the Anova on the side of the container and turn the clamp screw until it is tight.
- Fill the container to the fill line on the metal part of the Anova and press the power button. The display should light up with the temperature in either Celsius or Fahrenheit and this can be changed by pressing the "select" button.
- For your convenience, this book lists all temperatures in both Celsius and Fahrenheit.
- Simply roll the dial on the display to the desired temperature and press the "set" button. The circulator will activate and the water will begin to heat.
- Once it has reach the proper temperature, the Anova will beep to let you know that it's time to cook.

Sous Vide Isn't Just for Meat

As we'll discuss later in the recipes, sous vide cooking is an excellent way of ensuring that your meat dishes come out perfectly without worrying about how hot or how long to cook, but what you may not know is that the sous vide method can cook just about anything to perfection. Any vegetables that you would have either roasted or steamed can be sealed into a vacuum-sealed bag for a quick and easy sous vide that locks in all the valuable nutrients. And this way, your veggies are standing by and ready to eat whenever you are.

Sous Vide for Breakfast

Who isn't a fan of a perfectly cooked Eggs Benedict? But poached eggs can take a lot of practice to get just right. Since your sous vide maintains a constant temperature at all times, making the perfect poached egg is as easy as cracking an egg. The same method can be used to make soft boiled and hard boiled eggs as well. Just drop the egg into the water bath and set a kitchen timer. Your eggs will be the exact consistency you want every time.

Make Your Favorite Slow-Cooked Barbecue With Your Anova

If you're a fan of good old fashioned barbecue, you know that it's not easy. You'll need a smoker, a lot of time, and you need to check it constantly to make sure it's hot enough, or not too hot. It's pretty much a full time job. I know it sounds crazy, but what if you could make all of your favorite slow-cooked barbecue foods sous vide with hardly any work? As we'll discuss later in the book, some of these recipes require a long cooking time, but with a sous vide you won't have to keep checking on your food. You can safely start cooking in the morning, go to work, and have dinner waiting for you when you get home. And best of all, your food will be succulent and tender every single time.

6

Pro Tips to Make Perfect Sous Vide Creations

A Great Sear is a Way to Add Flavor

You've gotten your food to the desired temperature, but what's next? Well, certain foods like vegetables and fish are often ready to eat right out of the bag. But things like beef or chicken can benefit from one more step. If you're making a nice New York Strip steak, your sous vide has cooked the inside to whatever temperature you prefer, but most of us like a nice dark sear on a steak. Once you're happy with the internal temperature, get a pan (preferably a cast iron pan) hot to the point of smoking with a tablespoon of vegetable oil. Drop your steak in the pan for just a couple of minutes on each side to achieve a nice dark sear. To enhance the sear further, try putting a tablespoon of butter in the pan while searing for an even darker, crisper crust. The high heat will sear the outside nicely, but the inside will stay juicy and rare.

With The Anova There's No Need to Rest Meat

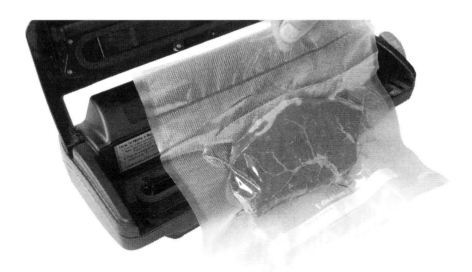

Generally, when cooking things like beef, you will need to rest it after cooking. Depending on how large a piece of meat you have, this time could range anywhere from ten minutes for an average steak, to about an hour for a rib roast. The reason meat needs to rest is to give the cooler internal temperature of the meat time to even out with the hotter external temperature of the surface of the meat. Allowing the meat to rest ensures that the juices within the meat will be fully absorbed and not lost when the meat is cut. When meat is cooked sous vide, this difference between the internal and external temperatures does not exist, which means meat cooked sous vide can be served right out of the bag. Or right out of the pan if you're searing it.

Cook Low and Slow for Fall-Off-The-Bone Meats

We've already discussed the fact that cooking sous vide is a great way to make your favorite barbecue dishes in your kitchen without the hassle of using a smoker, but how does this really work? Meats like pork shoulder and brisket are delicious, but in order to get that fall off the bone texture they have to be cooked for a long time. This means that you either have to smoke them at low temperatures or keep them in the oven all day. This can be tricky if you have a busy schedule. But with sous vide cooking you can safely cook food all day without supervision. If you want to make perfect pork ribs at home, season the outside of the meat with your favorite rub (we'll talk more about rubs later), seal it with your vacuum sealer, and adjust your Anova Immersion Circulator to 165 degrees. Then submerge the ribs in the water and cook for twelve hours.

Never Cook Too Low for Too Long

Sous vide cooking is one of the easiest and safest ways to cook almost anything, but if food is cooked at too low a temperature for too long, you run the risk of food borne illness. Foods like fish are best at around 120-125 degrees, but they only require around a half an hour in the sous vide to cook properly. After more than three hours at such a low temperature, bacteria can begin to multiply and become a health risk. A good rule of thumb is: Foods that are best at a low temp like fish should only cook for a short time (less than three hours), and foods that need a long cook time need to be cooked at high temperatures (165 degrees and up). If you stick to these basic guidelines you shouldn't ever have to worry about your food being 100% safe to eat.

Equipment Recommendations

We recommend the Anova Precision Cooker because it is affordable and compact enough to store easily. It has enough power to heat and circulate a large volume of water, but it isn't as bulky as models commonly used in restaurants. We also recommend a vacuum sealer—Foodsaver. It is the absolute best product for sealing your food, but with so many models available, it can be difficult to know which one is right for you. For home use, we recommend the Foodsaver V2244 which should offer the flexibility to seal anything, but is still affordable and won't take up too much room in your kitchen.

7

How to Store Your Leftover Sous Vide Items

General Storage

The best way to store your food is to use the Foodsaver (or other brand of vacuum sealer). Since you already use one for your sous vide, why not use it for storage too?

The great thing about the Foodsaver is that it can be used to seal everything from meats and veggies to dry goods. With durable BPA-free bags, you can seal anything and have the peace of mind that it will be secure for very long period of time. The high quality heat seal is the key to freshness because it does not degrade over time. With the Foodsaver, once it's sealed, it stays sealed.

The Foodsaver Makes Storage a Breeze

We've already discussed the advantages of cooking using the Foodsaver to vacuum seal food, but it is, without a doubt, the single best way to store leftovers either in the refrigerator or freezer. Simply follow the same steps with leftover food, and store in the freezer for months. Foodsaver bags are also easy to write on, so there's no guess work as to how long something has been in the freezer. And because your food has already been cooked to the perfect temperature, it is completely safe to reseal cooked food for freezing.

Use the Foodsaver to Turn Tonight's Leftovers into Next Week's Dinner

Since the Foodsaver along with the sous vide method makes cooking so easy, why not make extra food for those days when you just don't have time to cook but still want a delicious home cooked meal. If you plan ahead and sous vide more that you're planning to eat, just reseal the leftovers with your Foodsaver in the same bag you used to cook, and pop it in the freezer. When you're ready to use those leftovers, either thaw in the fridge or simply put the frozen bag back in your sous-vide at 165 degrees for about an hour. You now have another perfectly cooked meal with no work.

Store Your Sous Vide Items Together or Separately

Most people tend to store their leftovers in separate containers. Meat in one, mashed potatoes in another. With the Foodsaver you can seal your leftovers separately, or create complete meals that are ready to heat up whenever. It's like the ultimate TV dinner that you made yourself.

8

APPETIZERS

Sous Vide Duck Leg Confit

Servings: 2 | Prep time: 20 minutes | Cook time: 10-12 hours

Duck confit usually takes at least a whole day to prepare, but using your Anova you can make a delicious duck confit with hardly any effort at all.

Ingredients:

1 tablespoon dried thyme

3 bay leaves

1 cup salt

2 duck legs, frenched

6 tablespoons duck fat

Salt and freshly ground pepper, to taste

3 tablespoons duck fat

Instructions:

1. Crush the dried thyme and bay leaves in the salt until they are evenly mixed. Liberally coat the duck legs with the salt mixture and place in the refrigerator at least 12, and up to 36 hours.

2. Remove the duck legs from the refrigerator and rinse off the salt with cold water.

3. Set your Anova unit to 167F/75C.

4. Place the duck legs in a vacuum-sealed bag with 4 tablespoons of the duck fat and seal.

5. Once the water bath has reached the correct temperature, place the sealed bag in the water.

6. Cook the duck legs for 10 to 12 hours.

7. Remove the bag from the water and remove the duck legs from the bag.

8. When you are ready to serve, heat a pan with 2 tablespoons of duck fat and sear until the skin is crispy.

9.   Just before serving, in a hot pan, warm the remaining 2 tablespoons duck fat. Add the duck legs and sear until the skin is crisp.

10.   This process can also be used to cook duck breasts. Just adjust the temperature of the water bath to 135F/57C and cook for 45 minutes.

Nutritional Info: Calories: 665, Sodium: 82 mg, Dietary Fiber: 1.3 g, Total Fat: 62 g, Total Carbs: 3.1 g, Protein: 22 g.

Soft Sous Vide Goose Egg

Servings: 2 | Prep time: 30 minutes | Cook time: 2 1/2 hours

This decadent treat is an excellent start to any meal, and the rich polenta can also be used in many other recipes with amazing results.

Ingredients for the Polenta:

1 cup coarse ground polenta

6 tablespoons butter, divided

4 cups whole milk

1 cup parmesan, grated

Sea salt and freshly ground black pepper to taste

Instructions for the Polenta:

1. First, fill up your water bath and set your Anova unit to 190F/87C.

2. While the water is warming up, place the polenta, butter, and milk into a vacuum-sealed bag. Your vacuum sealer should remove all of the air from around the food.

3. Submerge the bag and cook for 2 to 2 1/2 hours. While the polenta cooks, grate 8 ounces of Parmesan cheese.

4. Remove the bag from the water oven and pour immediately over the Parmesan cheese in a large bowl. Toss the ingredients and season with salt and pepper.

Ingredients for the Pancetta and Eggs:

4 goose eggs that are similar in size (the size of the eggs will affect their cooking time)

8 slices of pancetta, preferably very thin

4 handfuls of your favorite greens, tossed with a little extra-virgin olive oil

A few pinches of sea salt

Freshly grated parmesan

Instructions for the Pancetta and Eggs:

1. Using the same water bath, adjust your Anova unit to 167F/75C. It'll take a little while for the water to cook down so you can also add a bit of cold water to the bath to speed up the process. You can keep the polenta warm in the water bath while you cook the pancetta and eggs. The average goose egg will need to cook for 5 minutes.

2. Gently place to eggs in the water bath. There is no need to seal them.

3. While the eggs cook, heat up a cast-iron or stainless steel skillet over medium heat and cook the pancetta until golden brown, about 5 to 7 minutes.

4. When browned, place pancetta on a plate and cover with a paper towel. Using a pair of tongs, pull the eggs from the water bath, and rinse under cold water. Since your eggs are very fragile, be careful when cracking them.

5. Spoon polenta onto a plate and place the egg in the middle of the polenta. Top with the crispy polenta and serve with greens and a generous dusting of grated Parmesan cheese.

Nutritional Info: Calories: 1,162, Sodium: 1,031 mg, Dietary Fiber: 2 g, Total Fat: 70 g, Total Carbs: 85 g, Protein: 49 g.

Sous Vide Salmon Gravlox

Servings: 8 | Prep time: 30 minutes | Cook time: 1 hour

Gravlox is generally requires a long time to achieve succulent cured salmon, but you can speed up the process with excellent results using your Anova.

Ingredients:

4 tablespoons salt

4 tablespoons sugar

1 teaspoon powdered smoke* (optional)

8 salmon portions

Instructions:

1. Set your Anova unit to 104F/40C.

2. Mix together the salt and sugar, and completely cover the salmon in the dry cure mixture. Let sit for 30 minutes, then rinse.

3. Put the salmon portions into vacuum-sealed bags (you can seal them individually or side by side, but don't stack them).

4. Submerge the bags in the water oven to cook for 45 minutes to 1 hour.

5. Remove the bags from the water bath and chill in an ice water bath for 15 to 20 minutes.

6. Serve as an appetizer or with toasted bagels, cream cheese, onions and capers for a traditional Scandinavian breakfast.

Nutritional Info: Calories: 258, Sodium: 78 mg, Dietary Fiber: 0 g, Total Fat: 11 g, Total Carbs: 6 g, Protein: 34.5 g.

Sous Vide Herb Butter Shrimp

Servings: 3 | Prep time: 10 minutes | Cook time: 20 minutes

Everyone loves shrimp but cooking them properly can be a challenge. It seems like they're either over or undercooked. Luckily, cooking shrimp sous vide takes all of the guess work out of perfectly cooked shrimp.

Ingredients:

12 medium peeled shrimps

1/4 melted butter

1 finely minced shallot

2 teaspoons fresh thyme

1/2 teaspoon grated lemon zest

1 tablespoon lemon juice, for serving

Instructions:

1. Fill your water bath and set your Anova to 125F/51.6C.

2. While the water is coming up to the proper temperature, place all of the ingredients in a vacuum-sealed bag.

3. Place the bag in the water bath and cook for 20 minutes. Do not cook the shrimp longer than 30 minutes for the texture will become mushy.

4. Remove the bag from the water and serve. The shrimp make a great appetizer on their own, or you can toss them with your favorite pasta. They can also be chilled and used in a salad.

Nutritional Info: Calories: 37, Sodium: 64 mg, Dietary Fiber: 0.9 g, Total Fat: 1.5 g, Total Carbs: 0.9 g, Protein: 5.3 g.

Sous Vide Prosciutto Wrapped Rabbit

Servings: 4 | Prep time: 20 minutes | Cook time: 5 hours

This dish may appear complicated, but using your Anova will make preparation and cooking easier than you can imagine. Impress your guests with something truly unique and extraordinary.

Ingredients:

- 1 pound rabbit hind leg meat, boned, diced large
- 1/4 pound bacon, diced
- 1/4 pound pork butt, diced
- 1/2 teaspoon each coriander, clove, fennel, and juniper berry, finely ground
- 1/4 cup brandy
- 1 teaspoon fresh marjoram, finely chopped
- 1 teaspoon fresh thyme, finely chopped
- 1/2 cup heavy cream
- 12 thin slices prosciutto
- 4 rabbit loins
- 1 tablespoon olive oil
- 6 to 8 ounces maitake or chanterelle mushrooms
- 1 bunch kale, finely chopped
- Salt and pepper to taste
- 4 ounces demi-glace for the sauce

Instructions:

1. Fill your water bath and set Anova unit to 164F/73.5C.

2. In a food processor, grind the bacon, pork butt, rabbit hind leg meat and herbs. Then add the cream, spices and brandy to the food processor and puree until you have the texture of a mousse.

3. Chill the mousse for 30 minutes so that it becomes firm.

4. Place the prosciutto slices onto of a sheet of plastic wrap approximately 12 inches long, so that the prosciutto overlaps and provides a 6-inch wide sheet to work with.

5. Spread the mousse over the sheet of prosciutto creating a 1/3-inch thick layer.

6. Place the rabbit loin in the center of the mousse and season lightly with salt.

7. Roll the prosciutto around the loin, so that the loin is no longer visible. Remove the plastic wrap as you go so that the roll remains stable. Then, using a new piece of plastic wrap the roll the whole thing, creating a cylinder. Make sure it is tightly wrapped.

8. Cut a vacuum-seal bag a few inches longer than the cylinder and vacuum seal with your Foodsaver or any vacuum sealer that you have in your kitchen.

9. Place your sealed bag in the water bath and cook for 4 hours. Make an ice bath, and once the bag has finished cooking remove from hot water bath and place in the ice water to keep it from cooking any further.

10. While the bag is cooling in the ice bath, heat a pan on the stove to high heat. Unwrap the cylinder and place in the hot pan, searing on all sides. While you are doing this, heat your oven to 350 degrees. Once the cylinder is browned place in a roasting pan and place in the oven for 6 minutes.

11. While the cylinder roasts, heat a skillet over medium high heat with olive oil and sauté the mushrooms and kale until tender, and warm the demi-glace. Season to taste with salt and pepper.

12. Remove cylinder from the oven and let rest for ten minutes before slicing. Serve with the mushrooms and kale.

Nutritional Info: Calories: 616, Sodium: 1,368 mg, Dietary Fiber: 1.2 g, Total Fat: 35 g, Total Carbs: 6.6 g, Protein: 63 g.

Sous Vide Spinach Artichoke Dip

Servings: 10 | Prep time: 15 minutes | Cook time: 1 hour

This easy to make appetizer is excellent for entertaining or as a snack. It is best paired with a fresh French baguette and a glass of dry white wine.

Ingredients:

2 cups grated parmesan cheese

10 ounces frozen, chopped spinach (thawed)

14 ounces artichoke hearts, chopped

2/3 cups sour cream

1 cup cream cheese

1/3 cup mayonnaise

2 teaspoons minced garlic

1 baguette sliced into rounds

Olive oil for brushing

Instructions:

1. Fill your water bath and set your Anova unit to 165F/73.8C.

2. In a medium bowl, combine the parmesan cheese, spinach, and artichoke hearts.

3. In another bowl, mix together the sour cream, cream cheese, mayonnaise, and garlic.

4. Combine all ingredients in a vacuum-sealed bag. Once the water bath has reached the proper temperature, place the bag in the water bath and cook at least one hour, and up to six hours.

5. When the dip is almost finished, heat your oven to 400 degrees and slice the baguette into half-inch-thick rounds. Place the rounds on a baking sheet and brush lightly with olive oil. Place rounds in the oven for about 15 minutes until lightly browned.

6.   Remove the dip from the water bath and serve with toasted baguette.

Nutritional Info: Calories: 260, Sodium: 337 mg, Dietary Fiber: 2.9 g, Total Fat: 21 g, Total Carbs: 10.6 g, Protein: 10 g.

Tender Sous Vide Buffalo Wings

Servings: 10 | Prep time: 15 minutes | Cook time: 1 hour 10 minutes

Buffalo wings are usually fried, but for a healthier wing with fall off the bone meat and a crispy skin, your Anova will give you exactly the flavor you're looking for without deep frying.

Ingredients:

12 chicken wings

1/2 cup all-purpose flour

1/4 teaspoon cayenne pepper

1 dash garlic powder

1/4 teaspoon salt

1/4 cup melted butter

1/4 cup hot pepper sauce

1 3/4 tablespoons vegetable oil

Instructions:

1. Fill your water bath and set your Anova unit to 170F/76.6C.

2. In a medium bowl, mix together the flour, cayenne pepper, garlic powder, and salt. Place the dry mixture in a vacuum-sealed bag. Shake the mixture and then add the chicken wings. Shake again to coat the wings and then add the vegetable oil. Seal the bag using your vacuum sealer.

3. Once the water bath has reached to correct temperature, place the bag in the water and cook at least 1 hour and up to 4 hours.

4. In another bowl combine the melted butter and hot sauce.

5. When you are almost finished cooking the wings in the water bath heat your oven to 450 degrees.

6. Remove wings from the water bath and dip wings in the butter-hot sauce mixture so they are coated. Place the wings on a baking sheet and cook in the oven until the outside of the wings are crispy.

7.   Serve with blue cheese dressing and cut veggies.

Nutritional Info: Calories: 303, Sodium: 225 mg, Dietary Fiber: 0 g, Total Fat: 18 g, Total Carbs: 6 g, Protein: 25.8 g.

Spicy Ginger Pork Lettuce Wraps

Servings: 12 | Prep time: 1 hour | Cook time: 1-4 hours

Lettuce wraps are a light healthy alternative, and this Asian inspired pork filling packs plenty of flavor without the extra calories.

Ingredients:

3/4 pounds ground pork

1 red bell pepper, finely diced

1 garlic clove, minced

1 tablespoon minced peeled ginger

1 tablespoon Thai sweet chili sauce

1 tablespoon Asian fish sauce

1 teaspoon Asian sesame oil

1 tablespoon plus 1 teaspoon grapeseed oil

1 (8-ounce) can whole water chestnuts, drained and diced

2 scallions, thinly sliced

2 tablespoons oyster sauce

2 tablespoons chopped cilantro

24 large lettuce leaves

Instructions:

1. In a medium bowl, combine the ground pork with the bell pepper, garlic, ginger, chili sauce, fish sauce, sesame oil, and 1 tablespoon of the grapeseed oil. Allow to marinate for 1 hour.

2. While the pork marinates, set your Anova unit to 165F/73.8C and allow the water bath to come to the correct temperature. Once the pork is marinated, place pork and seasonings in a vacuum-sealed bag.

3. Place the bag in the water bath for at least one hour and up to four hours.

4.   When the pork is nearly finished cooking, heat a pan or wok with one tablespoon of grapeseed or vegetable oil until hot. Toss in the water chestnuts, scallions, oyster sauce and cilantro and sauté for about three minutes.

5.   Open the vacuum-sealed bag and stir in the pork and seasonings and remove from heat.

6.   Divide the lettuce leaves and spoon in the pork mixture to serve.

Nutritional Info: Calories: 97, Sodium: 156 mg, Dietary Fiber: 0.5 g, Total Fat: 3 g, Total Carbs: 8.8 g, Protein: 8 g.

Sous Vide Wagyu Meatballs

Servings: 6 | Prep time: 20 minutes | Cook time: 1-4 hours

Wagyu is one of the most decadent cuts of beef available and your sous vide is sure to seal in all of the juices and flavor it has to offer. This recipe will show you some amazing seasonings that will make your wagyu even more spectacular.

Ingredients:

1 pound wagyu or ground beef

1/4 cup bread crumbs

3 ounces milk

1/2 teaspoon salt

1/4 teaspoon black pepper

1 large egg, beaten

1/2 shallot, peeled and diced

3 tablespoons chopped fresh parsley

1 tablespoon dried oregano

1 tablespoon garlic powder

3 tablespoons grated parmesan cheese

2 tablespoons vegetable oil

Instructions:

1. In a bowl, mix the ground meat with all other ingredients. Do not over mix too much or meatballs will become dense.

2. Form into balls that are about two inches in diameter.

3. Put the meatballs onto a tray and freeze them for an hour.

4. Once firm, place the meatballs in a vacuum-sealed bag.

5. Set your Anova for 135F/57C and place bag into the water bath for at least one hour and not more than four hours.

6.   Remove the meatballs from the water bath and serve.

Note: If you prefer a crisper meatball simply pat them dry and heat two tablespoons of oil in a pan. Sauté the meatballs for several minutes or until browned.

Nutritional Info: Calories: 240, Sodium: 318 mg, Dietary Fiber: 0.7 g, Total Fat: 12 g, Total Carbs: 6 g, Protein: 26 g.

Sous Vide Chinese Crispy Pork Belly

Servings: 8 | Prep time: 10 minutes | Cook time: 6 hours

This delicious traditional dish is deceptively easy to prepare and your sous vide takes all of the guess work out of cooking perfect pork belly.

Ingredients:

2 pounds pork belly (skin on)

2 steel or wood skewers

2 teaspoons salt

1 teaspoon white pepper

1 teaspoon five spice powder

1 teaspoon white pepper

3 tablespoons white vinegar

Instructions:

1. Set your Anova unit to 165F/73.8C

2. In a small bowl, combine the salt, white pepper and Chinese five spice power. Sprinkle half of the mixture generously to cover the pork belly. Do not use the spices on the fat side.

3. Place your pork belly in a vacuum-sealed bag.

4. Submerge the pork belly in the water bath for at least six and not more than eight hours. When the pork belly is finished cooking, remove from the water bath and remove from the bag.

5. Dry the pork belly completely and use the remaining half of the spice mixture to season the pork belly again.

6. Set your broiler to high and place the pork belly on a baking sheet.

7. Cook under the broiler for ten to twelve minutes or until skin has reached desired crispiness.

8. Remove from broiler and cut into small pieces.

Nutritional Info: Calories: 523, Sodium: 1832 mg, Dietary Fiber: 0.9 g, Total Fat: 30.5 g, Total Carbs: 0.6 g, Protein: 53 g.

9

VEGETABLES

Agnolotti with Artichoke Sauce

Servings: 4 | Prep time: 15 minutes | Cook time: 30 minutes

This recipe is an easy way to make your pasta and sauce all at once, and your Foodsaver will make storing leftovers really simple. If you can't fin Agnolotti you can just use ravioli instead.

Sauce Ingredients:

1 (9-ounce) package frozen artichoke hearts, thawed and coarsely chopped

1 cup frozen peas (do not thaw)

1 cup half-and-half

1 clove garlic, smashed

1/8 teaspoon red pepper flakes

1 teaspoon finely grated lemon zest

2 teaspoons fresh lemon juice

Salt

Sauce Instructions:

1. Combine the artichokes, half-and-half, garlic, red pepper flakes and 1/4 teaspoon salt in a vacuum-sealed bag.

2. Set your Anova to 165F/73.8C and put the bag in the water bath for 30 minutes.

Pasta Ingredients:

1 pound refrigerated cheese agnolotti (or ravioli)

1 cup grated parmesan cheese

1/4 cup fresh basil leaves, chopped

Pasta Instructions:

1. While the sauce is cooking, bring a pot of water to a boil and add the agnolotti. Drain the pasta, but retain 1/2 of the pasta water.

2. Heat a pan over medium heat, and when the sauce is finished in the Anova, remove the bag from the water and pour the contents into the skillet. Add the pasta and 1/2 cup of pasta water and stir to coat. Then add the parmesan cheese and stir. Serve topped with the chopped basil.

Nutritional Info: Calories: 525, Sodium: 1214 mg, Dietary Fiber: 7 g, Total Fat: 27.6 g, Total Carbs: 36 g, Protein: 475 g.

Sous Vide Glazed Baby Carrots

Servings: 6 | Prep time: 10 minutes | Cook time: 1 hour 10 minutes

Cooking carrots sous vide is quick and easy, but because the carrots are cooking in their own juices, they retain so much flavor.

Ingredients:

1 pound baby whole baby carrots

2 tablespoons unsalted butter

Freshly ground black pepper

1 tablespoon granulated sugar

Salt

Instructions:

1. Set your Anova to 183F/83.8C.

2. In a vacuum-sealed bag, combine the carrots, butter, sugar, and 1/2 teaspoon of salt and seal.

3. Submerge the bag in the water bath for one hour.

4. When the carrots are almost finished, heat a pan over high heat.

5. Empty the carrots into the pan and cook until the liquid from the bag thickens and becomes a glaze.

Nutritional Info: Calories: 68, Sodium: 86 mg, Dietary Fiber: 2.2 g, Total Fat: 3.9 g, Total Carbs: 8.2 g, Protein: 0.5 g.

Frittata with Asparagus, Tomato, and Fontina

Servings: 3 | Prep time: 10 minutes | Cook time: 1 hour

We've already discussed how the sous vide is perfect for cooking eggs to the perfect consistency, and this recipe will teach you how to make a frittata that will make any breakfast special.

Ingredients:

6 large eggs

2 tablespoons whipping cream

1/4 teaspoon freshly ground black pepper

1 tablespoon olive oil

1 tablespoon butter

12 ounces asparagus, trimmed, cut into 1/4 to 1/2-inch pieces

1 tomato, seeded, diced

2 teaspoons salt

3 ounces fontina, diced

Instructions:

1. Heat your Anova to 176F/80C.

2. While the water is coming up to temperature, heat a pan over medium heat adding the olive oil.

3. When oil is hot, add the asparagus, salt, pepper, and tomato. Sauté until the asparagus is tender and remove from heat.

4. Beat the eggs and pour into a vacuum-sealed bag. Add the contents of the pan along with the butter and diced fontina. Submerge the bag into the water and try to keep it flat on the bottom of the container.

5. Cook for one hour, and remove from the water bath. Cut the bag open and serve.

Nutritional Info: Calories: 383, Sodium: 2339 mg, Dietary Fiber: 2.7 g, Total Fat: 31 g, Total Carbs: 7 g, Protein: 23 g.

Curried Potatoes and Chickpeas

Servings: 8 | Prep time: 20 minutes | Cook time: 2 hours

This simple but flavorful dish goes well with many different proteins and is easy to make but packs complex and exotic flavors.

Ingredients:

1 1/2 pounds Yukon gold potatoes, peeled and cut into 3/4-inch chunks

3 tablespoons unsalted butter

1 1/2 teaspoons curry powder

1/4 teaspoon cayenne pepper

1 (15–ounce) can chickpeas, drained and rinsed

2 cups fried onions

1/2 cup plain Greek yogurt

1/4 cup chopped fresh cilantro, plus leaves for topping

2 tablespoons fresh lime juice

1 jalapeno pepper, thinly sliced

Salt

Instructions:

1. Set your Anova to 200F/93.3C. While the water is heating, heat 2 tablespoons of butter in a saucepan and fry the onions.

2. Add the cut potatoes, curry powder, cayenne pepper, chickpeas, and onions to a vacuum-sealed bag.

3. Submerge the bag in the water bath and cook for at least two hours and not more than four.

4. In a small bowl, combine the yogurt, cilantro, and lime juice. Remove the bag from the water bath and divide among small bowls. Top with the yogurt sauce and sliced jalapenos to serve.

Nutritional Info: Calories: 322, Sodium: 84 mg, Dietary Fiber: 11.3 g, Total Fat: 7.9 g, Total Carbs: 52.2 g, Protein: 13.3 g.

Sous Vide Mixed Vegetables

Servings: 6 | Prep time: 15 minutes | Cook time: 60-90 minutes

Sous vide is an excellent way of creating flavorful vegetable dishes. Feel free to experiment with whatever is in season.

Ingredients:

1 1/2 pounds mixed vegetables like yellow squash, zucchini, red and green peppers, eggplant)

2 tablespoons olive oil

2 tablespoons fresh herbs finely chopped (parsley, thyme and chives)

Salt and pepper, to taste

Instructions:

1. Heat your Anova bath to 183F/83C.
2. Wash, peel, and cut the vegetables into 1-inch pieces. Put all of the vegetables into a vacuum-sealed bag. Add the oil, herbs and salt and pepper to the bag before vacuum sealing.
3. Place the bags in the water and cook for about 60- 90 minutes.
4. Once cooked, serve immediately or chill the vegetables and use later. You can use them to make the following delicious recipes: Couscous with Mediterranean Vegetables, Vegetable Flatbread Wraps, or Hearty Vegetable Soup.

Nutritional Info: Calories: 81, Sodium: 255 mg, Dietary Fiber: 4.3 g, Total Fat: 5.0 g, Total Carbs: 8.2 g, Protein: 1.7 g.

Sous Vide Summer Salsa

Servings: 10 | Prep time: 10 minutes | Cook time: 30 minutes

Salsa isn't usually cooked, but using the low even heat of the sous vide to blend the flavors will add a new dimension to your salsa.

Ingredients:

2 cans of sweet corn (yellow or white)

1 can black beans

1/2 red onion, chopped

1 red bell pepper, chopped

1/2 cup sugar

1/2 cup rice wine vinegar (red wine or champagne vinegar will also work)

Salt

Instructions:

1. Set your Anova to 125F/51.6C and combine all the ingredients in a vacuum-sealed bag.

2. Seal the bag and submerge in the water bath for 30 minutes.

3. Remove bag from water and chill in the refrigerator for one hour before serving.

Nutritional Info: Calories: 155, Sodium: 2 mg, Dietary Fiber: 4.4 g, Total Fat: 0.6 g, Total Carbs: 32.3 g, Protein: 5.6 g.

Sous Vide Balsamic Beets

Servings: 6 | Prep time: 10 minutes | Cook time: 2 hours

Using your Anova is an excellent way to infuse the flavor of balsamic vinegar into beets for a flavor packed vegetable dish.

Ingredients:

6 medium beets (2 bunches, or about 3-1/2 pounds)

1 teaspoon salt

2 tablespoons extra virgin olive oil

1/3 cup inexpensive balsamic vinegar

1 tablespoon maple syrup

Freshly ground black pepper, to taste

Instructions:

1. Set your Anova to 185F/85C.
2. Place the chopped beets, olive oil, salt and two tablespoons of balsamic vinegar into a vacuum-sealed bag.
3. Submerge the bag in the water bath and cook for 2 hours.
4. While the beets are cooking, combine the remaining balsamic vinegar, and maple syrup in a small saucepan.
5. Heat on medium until the mixture has reduced slightly, making sure not to burn the vinegar.
6. Remove the beets from the water bath and transfer to a medium bowl. Pour balsamic reduction over the beets and stir to coat.

Nutritional Info: Calories: 74, Sodium: 427 mg, Dietary Fiber: 1 g, Total Fat: 4.8 g,

Total Carbs: 7.3 g, Protein: 0.8 g.

Spicy Butter Poached Asparagus

Servings: 4 | Prep time: 10 minutes | Cook time: 10-12 minutes

Add a kick to traditional asparagus for delicious results. Using your Anova to make vegetables gives you complete control over texture and flavor.

Ingredients:

1 bunch of asparagus, trimmed

3 tablespoons unsalted butter

1/2 teaspoon cayenne pepper

Pinch of salt

Instructions:

1. Set your Anova for 185F/85C.

2. Trim the bottoms of the asparagus and place them flat in a vacuum-sealed bag.

3. Melt the butter and add the cayenne pepper. Drizzle the spiced butter over the asparagus and use a vacuum sealer to seal the bag.

4. When the water bath has reached the proper temperature place the bag in the water and cook for 10 to 12 minutes.

5. Remove the bag from the water and sprinkle a pinch of salt on the asparagus before serving.

Nutritional Info: Calories: 78, Sodium: 61 mg, Dietary Fiber: 0 g, Total Fat: 9 g,

Total Carbs: 0.3 g, Protein: 0.2 g.

Sous Vide Root Vegetables with Brown Butter

Servings: 6 | Prep time: 30 minutes | Cook time: 3 hours

Root vegetables are a savory side, and cooking them sous vide will add even more earthy flavor.

Ingredients:

1 turnip, peeled and cut into pieces

8 baby carrots, peeled and cut into pieces

1 medium parsnip, peeled and cut into pieces

1/2 medium red onion, peeled and cut into pieces

4 cloves garlic, crushed

4 sprigs fresh rosemary, on the stem

2 tablespoons extra-virgin olive oil

2 tablespoons butter

salt and freshly ground pepper

Instructions:

1. Set your Anova to 185F/85C.
2. Combine all ingredients in a large vacuum-sealed bag.
3. Submerge the bag in the water bath and cook for 3 hours.
4. Remove the bag from the water bath and strain out the cooking liquid.
5. Heat a saucepan over medium heat and add the cooking liquid, reducing until it slightly thickens.
6. Pour the liquid over the vegetables to serve.

Nutritional Info: Calories: 114, Sodium: 55 mg, Dietary Fiber: 2.9 g, Total Fat: 8.9 g, Total Carbs: 9.2 g, Protein: 0.9 g.

Sous Vide Butternut Squash

Servings: 4 | Pre time: 10 minutes | Cook time: 1 hour

Butternut squash is full of hearty flavors that are only enhanced with sous vide cooking.

Ingredients:

1 butternut squash, peeled and cut into pieces

1 tablespoon butter

1 sprig fresh thyme

1 sprig fresh sage

1 teaspoon salt

1 tablespoon light brown sugar

Instructions:

1. Set your Anova to 155F/68C.
2. Place the diced squash, butter, herbs, and salt in a large vacuum-sealed bag.
3. Submerge in the water bath for 1 hour.
4. Remove from water bath and place on a baking sheet. Heat your oven to 400F.
5. Sprinkle the brown sugar over the squash and cook in the oven for 10 minutes.

Nutritional Info: Calories: 53, Sodium: 604 mg, Dietary Fiber: 1.1 g, Total Fat: 3.0 g, Total Carbs: 6.9 g, Protein: 0.5 g.

Sous Vide Maple Glazed Sweet Potatoes

Servings: 6 | Prep time: 10 minutes | Cook time: 60-90 minutes

Your Anova is an excellent way to cook sweet potatoes and lock in all of their delicious flavor.

Ingredients:

2 1/2 pounds sweet potatoes, peeled and cut into 1 1/2-inch pieces

1/3 cup pure maple syrup

2 tablespoons butter, melted

1 tablespoon lemon juice

1/2 teaspoon salt

Instructions:

1. Set your Anova to 190F/87.7C.

2. Combine all the ingredients in a vacuum-sealed bag.

3. Submerge the bag in the water bath and cook for at least 60 minutes and not longer than 90 minutes.

4. Remove from bag and drizzle the liquid over the potatoes to serve.

Nutritional Info: Calories: 303, Sodium: 240 mg, Dietary Fiber: 7.8 g, Total Fat: 4.2 g, Total Carbs: 64.5 g, Protein: 3.0 g.

10

CHICKEN

Sous Vide Bourbon Chicken

Servings: 4 | Prep time: 20 minutes | Cook time: 1 hour 10 minutes

This is a super easy recipe that packs a ton of flavor with hardly any work, and it doesn't even require any bourbon. It was originally created by a Chinese chef working on Bourbon Street in New Orleans.

Ingredients:

2 pounds boneless chicken breasts, cut into bite-size pieces

2 tablespoons olive oil

1 garlic clove, crushed

1/4 teaspoon ginger

3/4 teaspoons crushed red pepper flakes

1/4 cup apple juice

1/3 cup light brown sugar

2 tablespoons ketchup

1 tablespoon cider vinegar

1/2 cup water

1/3 cup soy sauce

Instructions:

1. Set your Anova to 150F/65.5C.

2. In a medium pan, heat the oil until hot but not smoking. Add the chicken and cook just until slightly browned. Remove chicken from heat.

3. Add the remaining ingredients and chicken to a vacuum-sealed bag.

4. Place the bag into the water bath and cook for one hour. This will give the ingredients time to combine into a flavorful sauce and finish cooking the chicken.

5. Remove the bag from the water bath and serve with steamed white or brown rice, or your choice of sous vide vegetables that can be cooked in a separate bag at the same time.

Nutritional Info: Calories: 566, Sodium: 1482 mg, Dietary Fiber: 0 g, Total Fat: 23.9 g, Total Carbs: 17.7 g, Protein: 67.2 g.

Sous Vide Chicken Teriyaki

Servings: 6 | Prep time: 10 minutes | Cook time: 1 hour

Your sous vide is a great way to make this Japanese favorite at home without all the excess oil that restaurants typically use.

Ingredients:

1 tablespoon cornstarch

1 tablespoon cold water

1/2 cup white sugar

1/2 cup soy sauce

1/4 cup cider vinegar

1 clove garlic, minced

1/2 teaspoon ground ginger

1/4 teaspoon ground black pepper

12 skinless chicken thighs

Instructions:

1. Set your Anova to 165F/73.8C.
2. In a small bowl, combine the cornstarch, cold water, sugar, soy sauce, vinegar, garlic, ginger and ground black pepper.
3. Add sauce mixture and chicken thighs to a vacuum-sealed bag.
4. When the water bath has reached the correct temperature, submerge the bag and cook for 1 hour.
5. Heat broiler to high.
6. Remove the bag from the bath and place chicken on a baking sheet and brush with sauce from the bag. Cook the chicken for 2 to 3 minutes on each side under the broiler to sear.
7. Serve with steamed white or brown rice, or sous vide vegetables.

Nutritional Info: Calories: 241, Sodium: 1270 mg, Dietary Fiber: 0 g, Total Fat: 6.2 g, Total Carbs: 19.9 g, Protein: 25.5 g.

Sous Vide Barbecue Chicken

Servings: 4 | Prep time: 10 minutes Cook time: 1 1/2 hours

For the most succulent chicken breasts, sous vide is the home cook's best friend. Never again worry that your chicken breasts will be overcooked and tough.

Ingredients:

4 chicken breasts

1 or 2 sprigs of fresh thyme

1 or 2 sprigs of fresh rosemary

1/2 teaspoon ancho pepper, or other chili powder

BBQ Sauce

Instructions:

1. Set your Anova for 141F/60C.

2. Season the chicken with salt and pepper and place them in a vacuum-sealed bag.

3. Add the rosemary and thyme to the bag and seal.

4. Place the bag in the water bath and cook for at least 1 1/2 hours and not more than 2 1/2.

5. When the chicken is almost finished cooking heat either your grill or broiler to high. Remove the chicken from the bag and pat dry with paper towels.

6. Slather with BBQ sauce and place them on the grill or under the broiler for just long enough to char the sauce. Serve immediately.

Nutritional Info: Calories: 123, Sodium: 62 mg, Dietary Fiber: 0 g, Total Fat: 4.8 g,

Total Carbs: 0.9 g, Protein: 18.1 g.

Sous Vide Tequila Lime Chicken

Servings: 4 | Prep time: 20 minutes | Cook time: 1 hour

Getting some char on chicken breasts can add a lot of flavor, but cooking breasts on the grill can also end up drying out the meat. Using your Anova and broiler, you can get all the flavor of the grill and still end up with juicy tender meat.

Ingredients:

3 tablespoons olive oil

3 tablespoons tequila

1 tablespoon lime zest, from about 2 limes

4 cloves garlic, minced

1 1/4 teaspoons ancho chili powder

1/2 teaspoon ground coriander

1/4 teaspoon dried oregano

1 1/4 teaspoons salt

1/2 teaspoon freshly ground black pepper

2 teaspoons honey

4 boneless skinless chicken breasts

1 lime, sliced into wedges, for serving

Instructions:

1. Set your Anova for 150F/65.5C

2. Season the chicken with salt and pepper and set aside.

3. Combine all of the other ingredients in a bowl and stir.

4. Place the chicken breasts in a vacuum-sealed bag, add 2/3 of the seasoning mixture, and seal. The vacuum-sealed bag will marinate the meat as it cooks.

5. Place in the water bath and cook for at least 1 hour and not more than 2.

6. When you are almost finished cooking, heat your boiler to high.

7.   Remove the chicken from the bag and pat dry with paper towels.

8.   Place on a baking sheet and baste with the remaining seasoning mixture.

9.   Cook under the broiler for just long enough for the chicken to char. Flip the chicken over and char that side.

10.   Serve immediately. This dish goes well with a fresh corn salad.

Nutritional Info: Calories: 131, Sodium: 775 mg, Dietary Fiber: 1.1 g, Total Fat: 3.4 g, Total Carbs: 6.6 g, Protein: 12.8 g.

Super Healthy Sous Vide Chicken Parmesan

Servings: 4 | Prep time: 15 minutes | Cook time: 1 hour

Chicken parmesan is usually fried, and that soaks up a lot of oil, but this simple recipe will show you how to get all of the flavor of classic chicken parmesan without worrying about extra calories.

Ingredients:

4 boneless, skinless chicken breasts

1/2 pound low moisture, whole milk mozzarella

1 28-ounce can whole, peeled tomatoes (preferably San Marzano)

3 cloves garlic, crushed

1 tablespoon fresh or dry oregano

1 tablespoon fresh chopped or dry basil

1 tablespoon extra-virgin olive oil

1 tablespoon lemon juice

2 teaspoons salt

Pinch of ground pepper

1 package spaghetti or linguini (for serving)

Grated parmesan (for serving)

Instructions:

1. Set your Anova to 150F/65.5C.

2. Season the chicken breasts with 1 teaspoon of salt and a pinch of black pepper.

3. Place the chicken in a vacuum-sealed bag, and cook the chicken in the water bath for at least 1 hour and not more than 2.

4. While the chicken is cooking, make the sauce.

5. In a food processor or blender, add the tomatoes, garlic, oregano, basil, and the remaining salt and pepper. Pulse several times until the tomatoes are chopped but not quite smooth.

6. Pour the contents of the food processor into a medium saucepan and add the olive oil.

7. Heat over medium heat, stirring frequently. When the sauce has darkened a bit add the lemon juice and remove from heat. This should take about 20 minutes.

8. Heat a pot of salted water on the stove. When boiling, add the spaghetti or linguini, cooking based on package directions, and drain.

9. Slice the mozzarella into 1/4-thick rounds.

10. Remove the chicken from the bag and pat dry with paper towels.

11. Arrange the chicken on a baking sheet and place the sliced mozzarella on top. Heat broiler to high and place the baking sheet in the broiler, cooking until the cheese is starting to melt and brown.

12. Remove chicken from broiler. Arrange pasta on plates and place chicken on the pasta.

13. To serve, top the chicken breasts with a liberal amount of tomato sauce, and grated parmesan cheese.

Nutritional Info: Calories: 383, Sodium: 93 mg, Dietary Fiber: 1.1 g, Total Fat: 11 g,

Total Carbs: 46.1 g, Protein: 25.4 g.

Sous Vide Crispy Drumsticks

Servings: 6 | Prep time: 10 minutes | Cook time: 1 hour

These drumsticks are moist and juicy on the inside thanks to your Anova's even heat.

Ingredients:

12 drumsticks	*Salt*
6 tablespoons vegetable oil	*Pepper*

Instructions:

1. Set your Anova to 158F/70C.

2. Season the drumsticks with salt and pepper and seal 4 in each vacuum-sealed bag.

3. Submerge the bags in the water bath and cook for one hour.

4. When the chicken is nearly finished cooking, heat a large skillet with the oil over medium-high heat.

5. Remove the chicken from the bags and cook quickly in the skillet until skin is crisp and golden brown.

Nutritional Info: Calories: 276, Sodium: 101 mg, Dietary Fiber: 0 g, Total Fat: 18.9 g, Total Carbs: 0.1 g, Protein: 25.3 g.

Sous Vide Turkey Leg

Servings: 2 | Prep time: 10 minutes | Cook time: 6-7 hours

A favorite at the county fair, turkey legs are easy to make at home using your Anova, and you're guaranteed to have the most tender meat possible.

Ingredients:

2 large turkey legs, about 1 pound each

3 tablespoons butter

4 large fresh sage leaves, crumpled by hand

1 large sprig of rosemary

2 garlic cloves, smashed and peeled

1/2 teaspoon salt

1/2 teaspoon freshly-ground black pepper

Instructions:

1. Set your Anova to 170F/77C.
2. Place turkey legs into a vacuum-sealed bag with the butter, sage, rosemary, garlic, salt and pepper, and seal.
3. Place the bag in the water bath and cook for 6 to 7 hours.
4. Remove the bag from the water bath and pour the melted butter from the bag into a bowl.
5. Discard the bag and all other contents.
6. Pour the butter into a large skillet and heat to high.
7. Sear the turkey legs until they are brown on all sides.

Nutritional Info: Calories: 951, Sodium: 1024 mg, Dietary Fiber: 2.9 g, Total Fat: 40.9 g, Total Carbs: 5.4 g, Protein: 133.8 g.

Brown Sugar-Garlic Chicken

Servings: 2 | Prep time: 10 minutes | Cook time: 1 hour

This simple recipe is a fun twist on chicken breast that adds lots of interesting flavor.

Ingredients:

4 teaspoons brown sugar

12 ounces boneless, skinless chicken breasts

1 clove garlic

2 tablespoons butter

Dash black pepper

Instructions:

1. Set your Anova for 150F/65.5C.
2. In a small sauce pan, melt the butter and add brown the clove of garlic.
3. Place the chicken in a vacuum-sealed bag and add the garlic butter as well as the black pepper and seal.
4. Place the bag in the water bath and cook for at least 1 hour and not more than 2.
5. When you are almost finished cooking the chicken, heat your broiler to high.
6. Remove the chicken from the bag and place on a baking sheet.
7. Sprinkle the brown sugar over the chicken and cook under the broiler for just a minute or two so that the sugar melts and creates a glaze on the chicken. This is excellent served with steamed rice or vegetables.

Nutritional Info: Calories: 450, Sodium: 230 mg, Dietary Fiber: 0 g, Total Fat: 24.1 g, Total Carbs: 6.4 g, Protein: 49.4 g.

Sous Vide Spicy Chicken Sliders

Servings: 8 | Prep time: 20 minutes | Cook time: 1 hour

These sliders are a fun way to pack lots of flavor into an easy to eat sandwich.

Ingredients:

1 pound ground chicken

Salt

Ground pepper

1 tablespoon cayenne pepper

1 tablespoon ground mustard seed

1 teaspoon dried oregano

1/3 cup bread crumbs

1 tablespoon vegetable oil

12 soft slider buns

Butter lettuce, for serving

Instructions:

1. Set your Anova for 150F/65.5C.
2. In a large bowl, combine the chicken, salt, pepper, mustard, cayenne pepper, oregano, and bread crumbs. Mix well and make small patties.
3. Place the patties in a single layer in a vacuum-sealed bag.
4. Submerge in the water bath and cook for 1 hour.
5. When the chicken is almost finished cooking, heat a large skillet with the oil over medium heat.
6. Sear each patty for 1 minute per side and serve on the slider buns topped with lettuce.

Nutritional Info: Calories: 218, Sodium: 224 mg, Dietary Fiber: 1.4 g, Total Fat: 5.6 g, Total Carbs: 20.3 g, Protein: 20.6 g.

Sous Vide Vietnamese Chicken Wings

Servings: 6 | Prep time: 10 minutes | Cook time: 1 hour

These wings are easy to make and packed with flavor. Cooking them sous vide rather than on the grill will ensure that they stay moist and juicy.

Ingredients:

4 cloves minced garlic

1/4 cup lime juice

1/4 cup fish sauce

2 tablespoons soy sauce

3 tablespoons brown sugar

2 tablespoons vegetable oil

2 pounds chicken wings

Sprig of cilantro (for serving)

3 tablespoons sliced chilies (for serving)

Instructions:

1. Set your Anova for 170F/76.6C.
2. In a small bowl, combine all ingredients except the chicken wings.
3. Place the wings in a vacuum-sealed bag, pour in the marinade, and seal. For extra flavorful wings, place the bag in the refrigerator for a few hours.
4. Submerge the bag in the water bath and cook for at least 1 hour and up to 4 hours. When you are almost finished cooking, heat your broiler to high.
5. Remove the wings from the bag and discard the cooking liquid.
6. Place the wings on a baking sheet and cook under the broiler for a few minutes to slightly char the wings.
7. To serve, garnish with cilantro and sliced chilies.

Nutritional Info: Calories: 370, Sodium: 474 mg, Dietary Fiber: 1.1 g, Total Fat: 16.2 g, Total Carbs: 8.8 g, Protein: 44.8 g.

Sous Vide Crispy Chicken Thighs

Servings: 6 | Prep time: 5 minutes | Cook time: 1 hour

These are without a doubt; the most tender chicken thighs you've ever had. The crispy skin is just the icing on the cake.

Ingredients:

6 boneless, skin-on chicken thighs

salt and freshly ground pepper, to taste

2 garlic cloves, lightly smashed with a knife

2 or 3 fresh thyme sprigs

2 tablespoons unsalted butter

2 tablespoons canola oil, plus more as needed

Instructions:

1. Set your Anova for 150F/65.5C

2. Season the meat side of the chicken thighs with salt and pepper, then seal in vacuum-sealed bag.

3. Place the bag into the water bath and cook for at least 1 hour and not more that 2 hours.

4. When finished cooking, remove the chicken from the bag and place on a baking sheet. Place the baking sheet in the refrigerator for one hour.

5. Just before you're ready to serve, remove the chicken from the refrigerator and dry with paper towels.

6. Heat 2 tablespoon of oil in a medium skillet and cook the thighs skin side down until crisp. This should take about 8 minutes. Remove from the pan and serve immediately to maintain crispy skin. Do not cover or the skin will become soggy.

Nutritional Info: Calories: 157, Sodium: 64 mg, Dietary Fiber: 0 g, Total Fat: 11.6 g, Total Carbs: 0.7 g, Protein: 12.2 g.

Sous Vide Chicken with Sun Dried Tomato Vinaigrette

Servings: 4 | Prep time: 15 minutes | Cook time: 90 minutes

This easy to make chicken dish is packed with complex flavors and just the right amount of heat to keep things exciting.

Ingredients:

4 skin-on chicken breasts,

salt and fresh ground black pepper

1 poblano pepper

1/2 cup oil-packed sun-dried tomatoes, drained and chopped

2 tablespoons of oil from tomatoes

1 teaspoon honey

1/2 teaspoon soy sauce

2 teaspoons lemon juice

1 medium shallot, minced

1 tablespoon vegetable oil

Instructions:

1. Set your Anova to 150F/65C.

2. Season the chicken breasts with salt and pepper in a vacuum-sealed bag.

3. In another vacuum-sealed bag combine the poblano, sun-dried tomatoes, oil, honey, soy sauce, lemon juice, and shallot.

4. Submerge both bags in the water bath and cook for 90 minutes.

5. When almost finished cooking, heat a medium skillet over medium heat and add the vegetable oil.

6. Remove chicken from the vacuum-sealed bag and sear, skin side down until skin is crispy.

7.   Divide the chicken onto plates and top with warm tomato mixture.

Nutritional Info: Calories: 197, Sodium: 80 mg, Dietary Fiber: 0.8 g, Total Fat: 13.7 g, Total Carbs: 5.1 g, Protein: 13.8 g.

Sous Vide Chicken and Dumplings

Servings: 4 | Prep time: 15 minutes Cook time: 1 1/2 hours

This traditional country style recipe can also be made in a slow cooker, but for faster results use your Anova.

Ingredients:

4 skinless boneless chicken breasts

2 tablespoons butter

1 onion, diced

2 packages of refrigerated biscuit dough

2 cans of cream of chicken soup

Instructions:

1. Set your Anova to 155F/68.3C.

2. Place the chicken, butter, onion, and soup in a vacuum-sealed bag.

3. Submerge the bag in the water bath and cook for 2 hours.

4. When the bag containing the chicken has cooked for 1 1/2 hours, tear the biscuit dough into small pieces and place in a different vacuum-sealed bag.

5. Submerge the bag with the biscuit dough in the water bath and cook for 30 minutes.

6. Remove both bags at the same time, combine and serve.

Nutritional Info: Calories: 346, Sodium: 1263 mg, Dietary Fiber: 0.8 g, Total Fat: 20.7 g, Total Carbs: 22 g, Protein: 17.7 g.

Sous Vide Chicken Liver Mousse

Servings: 6 | Prep time: 20 minutes | Cook time: 90 minutes

The secret to amazing mousse is keeping the livers from overcooking. Luckily, your sous vide takes all of the guess work out of maintaining an even temperature.

Ingredients:

3 shallots, minced

2 sprigs fresh thyme

8 ounces cognac

1 pound chicken livers

4 large eggs

1/4 cup heavy cream

2 teaspoons salt

Instructions:

1. Set your Anova to 155F/68C.

2. In a large pan over medium heat, combine the shallots, and thyme, and cook until the shallots are beginning to caramelize. Remove from heat.

3. In a food processor, combine the cognac, chicken livers, eggs, and heavy cream, and blend until smooth.

4. Then add the shallots and thyme and pulse the food processor several times.

5. Place the mixture in a vacuum-sealed bag and submerge in the water bath for 90 minutes.

6. Remove from the water bath and place in the refrigerator for 1 hour to cool before serving.

Nutritional Info: Calories: 282, Sodium: 883 mg, Dietary Fiber: 0 g, Total Fat: 10.2 g, Total Carbs: 2.8 g, Protein: 23 g.

11

FISH

Sous Vide Spinach and Rice Stuffed Trout

Servings: 2 | Prep time: 15 minutes | Cook time: 45 minutes

Whole trout are tasty and delicate, and this recipe will teach you how to make an entire meal with just your Anova.

Ingredients:

2 whole trout, heads and tails removed

1/2 cup white parboiled rice

1/2 pound spinach, chopped

1 tablespoon garlic, finely chopped

1 teaspoon onion powder

2 tablespoons butter, melted

Salt & pepper to taste

Instructions:

1. Set your Anova to 130F/54.4C.
2. In a large bowl, combine the rice, spinach, garlic, onion powder and butter. Stir well.
3. Salt and pepper the insides of the trout and then stuff with the rice and spinach mixture.
4. Place the stuffed trout in separate vacuum-sealed bags. Because your Vacuum sealer creates a perfect seal it will keep the stuffing inside the fish as it cooks.
5. Submerge the bags in the water and cook for 45 minutes.
6. Remove the bags from the water and serve the fish with the stuffing still inside.

Nutritional Info: Calories: 426, Sodium: 294 mg, Dietary Fiber: 3.4 g, Total Fat: 17.6 g, Total Carbs: 43.8 g, Protein: 23.6 g.

Sous Vide Black Cod Filets

Servings: 2 | Prep time: 15 minutes | Cook time: 20 minutes

Black cod is the fattiest and most tender of all cods, and cooking it sous vide guarantees perfect texture.

Ingredients:

1 pound of black cod fillets, skin-on and scaled

3 tablespoons butter

3 sprigs of thyme

3 tablespoons salt

1 cup of water

Lemon wedges

Instructions:

1. Set your Anova to 125F/51.6C.

2. In a large bowl, combine the water, salt and cod filets. Allow them to brine for 10 minutes, then rise the fish thoroughly with cold water.

3. Place the filets in separate vacuum-sealed bags with 1 tablespoon butter and one sprig of thyme per bag.

4. Seal the bags and place in the water bath for 20 minutes.

5. When the fish is nearly cooked, heat your broiler to low.

6. Remove the fish from the bags and place on a backing rack, skin side up, and broil for 5 minutes, or until the skin is crispy.

7. Serve immediately to preserve crispy skin.

Nutritional Info: Calories: 404, Sodium: 306 mg, Dietary Fiber: 1.7 g, Total Fat: 19.6 g, Total Carbs: 2.9 g, Protein: 52.4 g.

Sous Vide Scrambled Eggs with Smoked Salmon

Servings: 3 | Prep time: 15 minutes | Cook time: 30 minutes

Eggs and salmon go together wonderfully, and your Anova can cook scrambled eggs to perfection.

Ingredients:

6 large eggs

2 tablespoons fresh chives, chopped

1/2 pound thin sliced smoked salmon

1/2 cup crème fraiche or sour cream

4 cups baby spinach or arugula

3 tablespoons extra virgin olive oil

2 tablespoons champagne vinegar

Salt

Black pepper

Instructions:

1. Set your Anova to 165F/73C.

2. In a bowl, whisk eggs together until smooth. Add the salt and pepper.

3. Pour eggs into a vacuum-sealed bag.

4. Place the bag into the water bath and set a timer for 10 minutes. When the timer goes off, remove the bag from the water and massage the bag to break up the eggs.

5. Place the bag back in the water bath and cook for another 10 minutes. Remove the bag and massage again before placing the bag back in the water bath for a final 10 minutes.

6. Remove the bag from the water, massage once more and divide the eggs on plates.

7. To make the salad, combine the olive oil and vinegar with a pinch of pepper and toss with the greens.

8. Top the eggs with chopped chives and slices of salmon. Then top the salmon with a dollop of crème fraiche and serve.

Nutritional Info: Calories: 461, Sodium: 227 mg, Dietary Fiber: 1.4 g, Total Fat: 36.9 g, Total Carbs: 5.1 g, Protein: 29.9 g.

Sous Vide Parmesan Tilapia

Servings: 4 | Prep time: 10 minutes | Cook time: 20 minutes

Tilapia is a sweet and delicate whitefish that is easy to overcook with traditional methods. This recipe will show you how to make perfectly flaky fish with a flavorful topping.

Ingredients:

1/2 cup parmesan cheese

1/4 cup butter, softened

3 tablespoons mayonnaise

2 tablespoons fresh lemon juice

1/4 teaspoon dried basil

1/4 teaspoon ground black pepper

1/8 teaspoon onion powder

1/8 teaspoon celery salt

2 pounds tilapia fillets

2 tablespoons olive oil

Instructions:

1. Set your Anova to 132F/55.5C.

2. Place Tilapia filets in a vacuum-sealed bag with the olive oil, seal and submerge in the water bath for 20 minutes.

3. In a small bowl, mix together the Parmesan cheese, butter, mayonnaise and lemon juice.

4. Season with dried basil, pepper, onion powder and celery salt. Mix and set aside.

5. When the tilapia is finished cooking, remove from the water bath and arrange filets on a baking sheet.

6. Heat your broiler to high, and top the fish with the cheese mixture.

7.   Cook under the broiler for just 2 or 3 minutes to brown the cheese and serve.

Nutritional Info: Calories: 394, Sodium: 242 mg, Dietary Fiber: 0 g, Total Fat: 24.3 g, Total Carbs: 3.0 g, Protein: 42.5 g.

Sous Vide Mediterranean Halibut

Servings: 2 | Prep time: 10 minutes | Cook time: 30 minutes

Halibut is a flaky yet meaty fish that needs to be cooked to the perfect temperature. Luckily, your Anova takes all the guess work out of perfectly cooked fish every time.

Ingredients:

1 teaspoon extra-virgin olive oil

1 small onion, thinly sliced

2 tablespoons dry white wine

1 clove garlic, finely chopped

1 cup canned diced tomatoes

4 Kalamata olives, pitted and chopped

1/8 teaspoon dried oregano

1/8 teaspoon freshly grated orange zest

1/4 teaspoon salt, divided

1/4 teaspoon freshly ground pepper, divided

8 ounces thick-cut, Pacific Halibut filets

Instructions:

1. Set your Anova to 132F/55.5C.

2. Heat oil in a medium nonstick skillet over medium-high heat. Add onion and cook, stirring often, until lightly browned, 2 to 4 minutes.

3. Add wine and garlic and simmer for 30 seconds. Stir in tomatoes, olives, oregano and orange zest. Season with 1/8 teaspoon salt and 1/8 teaspoon pepper.

4. Season the halibut with salt and pepper and place the halibut in a vacuum-sealed bag. Submerge in the water bath for 30 minutes.

5. Remove the fish from the water bath and top with the tomato mixture. Serve with steamed white or brown rice, or sous vide vegetables.

Nutritional Info: Calories: 339, Sodium: 978 mg, Dietary Fiber: 2.8 g, Total Fat: 17.5 g, Total Carbs: 27.7 g, Protein: 18.0 g.

Sous Vide Salmon Croquettes

Servings: 6 | Prep time: 20 minutes | Cook time: 20 minutes

Croquettes are an elegant and delicate way to prepare salmon, and your Anova makes achieving the perfect texture a breeze.

Ingredients:

1 cup soft bread crumbs

1 tablespoon Dijon mustard

1/4 teaspoon pepper

8 medium green onions, finely chopped

2 eggs, slightly beaten

1 pound salmon filet

2 tablespoons margarine or butter

Instructions:

1. Set your Anova to 125F/51.6C.

2. Place the salmon filet in a vacuum-sealed bag.

3. Submerge the bag in the water bath and cook for 15 to 20 minutes.

4. Remove the salmon from the bag and place in a large bowl. With a fork, shred the salmon into small pieces.

5. Combine all of the ingredients except for the butter with the salmon and mix thoroughly.

6. Heat a large skillet over medium heat, and melt the butter.

7. Using large spoons, form the salmon mixture into balls or patties about 2 to 3 inches across.

8. When the butter is hot, place the patties into the pan and cook until just browned.

9. Remove from the pan and serve with fresh greens.

10. Tip: these croquettes can also be made into sandwiches. Simply serve each one on a slider bun for a delicious two-bite sandwich.

Nutritional Info: Calories: 179, Sodium: 171 mg, Dietary Fiber: 0.8 g, Total Fat: 10.2 g, Total Carbs: 4.8 g, Protein: 17.5 g.

Sous Vide Salmon Steaks with Tarragon-Lemon Aioli

Servings: 4 | Prep time: 30 minutes | Cook time: 1 hour

Salmon steaks are most commonly done on the grill, but to maximize flavor and get the best texture, try this easy sous vide recipe.

Ingredients:

4 thick cut salmon steaks

2 tablespoons olive oil

1/2 cup mayonnaise

1 tablespoon dried tarragon

3 tablespoons lemon juice

3 tablespoons Dijon mustard

Salt

Black pepper, finely ground

3 tablespoons granulated sugar

Instructions:

1. Set your Anova to 130F/54.4C.

2. We're going to brine these steaks because it will help reduce the presence of albumin, that unpleasant white stuff that seeps out of salmon.

3. To do this, mix equal parts sugar and salt and coat the salmon steaks completely.

4. Place the steaks in the refrigerator for 10 to 20 minutes and then rinse off the salt and sugar. This should also help the meat stay nice and firm while it cooks.

5. Place the steaks in separate vacuum-sealed bags, and submerge in the water bath.

6. Cook for one hour.

7.   While the salmon cooks, mix the mayo, tarragon, lemon juice, and mustard in a bowl. Feel free to add a grind or two of pepper if you like.

8.   When the salmon is finished cooking, you can either serve it with the aioli as is or heat a pan with 2 tablespoons of olive oil over high heat or give the steaks a quick sear—not more than 2 minutes per side.

9.   Spoon a dollop of the aioli on top and serve.

Nutritional Info: Calories: 456, Sodium: 423 mg, Dietary Fiber: 0.5 g, Total Fat: 28.4 g, Total Carbs: 17.3 g, Protein: 35.5 g.

Sous Vide Haddock with Charmoula Sauce

Servings: 4 | Prep time: 20 minutes | Cook time: 30 minutes

Charmoula sauce is a rich Moroccan sauce that will liven up any dish.

Ingredients for Fish:

2 pounds fresh skinless haddock

2 tablespoons olive oil

2 green bell peppers, cut in slices

2 roma tomatoes, cut into rounds

2 tablespoons lemon juice

Ingredients for Charmoula Sauce:

1/2 cup coarsely chopped fresh cilantro

1/2 cup coarsely chopped fresh flat-leaf parsley

5 garlic cloves, coarsely chopped

1/3 cup fresh lemon juice

2 teaspoons sweet paprika

2 teaspoons salt

1 1/2 teaspoons ground cumin

1/4 teaspoon cayenne

1/2 cup olive oil

Instructions:

1. Set your Anova to 132F/55.6 C.
2. Arrange the haddock in a vacuum-sealed bag so that it is one layer. Then add the sliced peppers and tomatoes to the bag. Drizzle in the olive oil and seal.
3. Submerge the bag in the water bath and cook for 30 minutes.

4.   While the fish cooks, combine the sauce ingredients in the bowl of a food processor and puree. Add in the olive oil as you puree the rest of the ingredients.

5.   When the fish is finished cooking, remove it from the water bath and serve the fish on a bed of the peppers and tomatoes and topped with the sauce.

Nutritional Info: Calories: 1031, Sodium: 1181 mg, Dietary Fiber: 3.0 g, Total Fat: 33.1 g, Total Carbs: 9.4 g, Protein: 2.1 g.

Sous Vide Salmon and Broccoli Tagliatelle

Servings: 4 | Prep time: 20 minutes | Cook time: 30 minutes

This delicious and healthy dish is easy to make, and thanks to your Vacuum sealer, it's also easy to store leftovers.

Ingredients:

1 package dry tagliatelle

2/3 pounds broccoli, cut into small pieces

1 pound skinless, boneless salmon filets, cut into chunks

1/2 cup dry white wine

2 tablespoons butter

1 cup onion, thinly sliced

2/3 heavy cream

1 tablespoon fresh dill, for garnish

Salt & pepper to taste

Instructions:

1. Set your Anova for 130F/54.4C.

2. Boil a large pot of salted water.

3. Chop the salmon into two inch chunks, place in a vacuum-sealed bag with the wine, onion, butter and broccoli. Then seal and submerge in the water bath, cooking for 30 minutes.

4. While the salmon and broccoli cook, put the tagliatelle in the boiling water and cook based on package directions and drain, reserving 1/2 cup of the cooking liquid.

5. When salmon and pasta are both finished cooking, heat a large saucepan over medium heat and combine the pasta with the salmon mixture.

6. Add the reserved pasta water and the heavy cream. Simmer for several minutes until the sauce has thickened slightly and coated the pasta and fish.

7. This recipe may be too much food for two people so if there are any leftovers, just place everything in a vacuum-sealed bag.

8. When ready to eat again, simply set your Anova to 130F/54.4C and reheat for 30 minutes.

Nutritional Info: Calories: 428, Sodium: 175 mg, Dietary Fiber: 2.8 g, Total Fat: 21.2 g,
Total Carbs: 27.5 g, Protein: 28.8 g.

Sous Vide Fish Tacos with Pineapple Salsa

Servings: 6 | Prep time: 15 minutes | Cook time: 30 minutes

This refreshing fish taco recipe is full of bright flavors and just the right amount of spice. Thanks to your Anova, it is guaranteed to come out tender and juicy.

Ingredients:

1 1/2 pounds cod

1/2 teaspoon adobo seasoning

1/2 teaspoon chili powder

1/2 fresh pineapple

1 teaspoon sugar

1 tablespoon red onion, chopped

2 tablespoons cilantro, chopped

Juice of 1 lime

Salt

1 tablespoon vegetable oil

12 soft flour or corn tortillas

1 avocado, sliced

2 tablespoons sour cream

Instructions:

1. Set your Anova to 135F/57.2C.

2. Season the fish with the adobo seasoning and chili powder.

3. Place the fish in vacuum-sealed bags and submerge in the water bath for 30 minutes.

4. While the fish is cooking, dice the pineapple and mix with the sugar, onion, lime juice, cilantro and a pinch of chili powder.

5. When the fish is almost finished cooking, heat a pan over medium heat.

6. Remove the fish from the water and cook in the pan until just browned.

7. Remove from heat and chop the fish.

8. Heat the tortillas until warm, and top with fish.

9. Serve the salsa either on the side or on top of the fish for a festive taco dinner.

Nutritional Info: Calories: 335, Sodium: 145 mg, Dietary Fiber: 5.9 g, Total Fat: 12.1 g, Total Carbs: 28.5 g, Protein: 29.6 g.

Sous Vide Prawns
with Spicy Peanut Noodles

Servings: 4 | Prep time: 20 minutes | Cook time: 30 minutes

Spice up traditional pasta and shrimp with this easy Asian inspired dish. Best of all, the noodles can be made ahead of time and chilled for a refreshing summer dinner.

Ingredients:

1 pound large prawns or shrimp, peeled and deveined

2 cloves garlic, crushed

1 teaspoon cayenne pepper

1 tablespoon cilantro, chopped

2 tablespoon lemon juice

Salt

Ground black pepper

1 package spaghetti

2 tablespoons creamy peanut butter

2 tablespoons toasted sesame oil

2 tablespoons vegetable oil

Instructions:

1. Set your Anova to 149F/65C.

2. Place prawns in a vacuum-sealed bag with the garlic, cilantro, lemon juice, salt, and pepper.

3. Submerge in the water bath and cook for 15 minutes.

4. While the prawns cook, heat a pot of salted water to boiling and add the spaghetti. Cook according to package directions, run under cold water until the noodles are cool, and drain.

5. In a large bowl mix together the noodles with the peanut butter, sesame oil, and cayenne pepper. If you prefer more heat, add

another pinch of cayenne pepper. Chill in the refrigerator for 20 minutes.

6.   When the prawns are finished in the water bath, heat a skillet with the vegetable oil to high heat, and quickly sear the shrimp for no more than 30 seconds.

7.   Remove from heat and serve the prawns on a bed of the cold noodles.

Nutritional Info: Calories: 488, Sodium: 332 mg, Dietary Fiber: 0.7 g, Total Fat: 21.1 g, Total Carbs: 38.4 g, Protein: 35.1 g.

Sous Vide Sea Scallops

Servings: 4 | Prep time: 10 minutes | Cook time: 30 minutes

Diver scallops are delicious but they can be a challenge. This recipe will teach you to make foolproof scallops using your Anova.

Ingredients:

12 large sea scallops

1 tablespoon olive oil

1 tablespoons butter

Salt and pepper

Instructions:

1. Set your Anova to 123F/51C.

2. Place the scallops in a single layer inside a vacuum-sealed bag.

3. Submerge the bag in the water bath and cook for 30 minutes. This won't completely cook the scallops which is good because we're going to sear them in a pan.

4. When the scallops are finished in the water bath, heat a large stainless steel pan on high heat and add the butter.

5. Remove the scallops from the bag and dry completely with paper towels. This is necessary in order to get a good sear.

6. When the pan is almost smoking, add the scallops and sear for 20 seconds on each side.

7. Remove from the pan and serve immediately.

Nutritional Info: Calories: 135, Sodium: 165 mg, Dietary Fiber: 0 g, Total Fat: 7.1 g, Total Carbs: 2.1 g, Protein: 15.1 g.

Sous Vide Miso Cod

Servings: 2 | Prep time: 20 minutes | Cook time: 30 minutes

Miso paste is an excellent way to add complex flavor to many dishes. This recipe will show you how to make your cod really come alive.

Ingredients:

1 pound pacific or black cod

1/3 cup white miso paste

3 tablespoons mirin (Japanese cooking wine)

2 tablespoons rice vinegar

2 tablespoons brown sugar

1 bunch bok choy

2 tablespoons olive oil

Salt and pepper

Instructions:

1. Set your Anova to 132F/55.6C.

2. In a small bowl, combine the miso paste, mirin, rice vinegar, and brown sugar. Mix together and reserve 3 tablespoons for later.

3. Season the fish with salt and pepper and seal in a vacuum-sealed bag. Submerge the bag in the water bath and cook for 30 minutes.

4. In a medium skillet, heat the olive oil over high heat.

5. When the fish is finished cooking, remove from the water bath.

6. When the oil is hot, toss in the bok choy along with the reserved miso mixture and cook just until the bok choy begins to wilt. Divide the bok choy onto plates and top with the cod.

Nutritional Info: Calories: 522, Sodium: 2012 mg, Dietary Fiber: 3.3 g, Total Fat: 18.9 g, Total Carbs: 23.4 g, Protein: 58.3 g.

Sous Vide Ahi Tuna Steaks

Servings: 2 | Prep time: 10 minutes | Cook time: 30 minutes

By gently cooking Ahi tuna in your Anova you can achieve a wonderful balance of flavor and texture. The ponzu sauce adds a refreshing citrus twist on traditional soy sauce that livens up many dishes.

Ingredients:

1/3 cup honey

1/4 cup ponzu sauce

1 pound ahi tuna

2 cups short grain rice, for serving

1 tablespoon toasted sesame seeds, for serving

Instructions:

1. Set your Anova to 120F/48.9C.

2. In a small bowl, combine the honey and ponzu sauce.

3. Place the ahi steaks in a vacuum-sealed bag and add the honey and ponzu mixture.

4. Seal the bag and submerge in the water bath for 30 minutes.

5. While the tuna cooks, prepare the rice and add the sesame seeds.

6. Remove the tuna from the water bath, slice, and serve immediately with the rice.

Nutritional Info: Calories: 1305, Sodium: 805 mg, Dietary Fiber: 3.0 g, Total Fat: 21.8 g, Total Carbs: 197.5 g, Protein: 74.3 g.

12

LAMB

Sous Vide Spiced Lamb Kebabs

Servings: 4 | Prep time: 15 minutes | Cook time: 1 1/2 hours

With your sous vide, you don't need a grill to make tasty and juicy kebabs. Simply follow these steps and unlock an entirely new way to make this middle eastern favorite.

Ingredients:

2 garlic cloves, minced

Sea salt

freshly ground black pepper

1 teaspoon dried oregano

1 tablespoon olive oil

4 lamb steaks cut into 2 inch chunks

2 red peppers, deseeded and cut into chunks

1 large onion, cut into chunks

2 lemons, cut into wedges

6 steel or bamboo skewers

Instructions:

1. Set your Anova to 140F/60C.

2. In a large bowl combine the garlic, salt, pepper, oregano, olive oil, and lamb chunks. Stir thoroughly to coat.

3. Spoon the lamb into a vacuum-sealed bag.

4. Submerge in the water bath and cook for 1 1/2 hours.

5. When the lamb is almost finished cooking, heat your oven to 500F.

6. Remove the bag from the water and pat lamb dry with a paper towel.

7. Skewer the lamb, alternating lamb, pepper, and onion chunks.

8. Arrange the skewers on a baking sheet and cook in the oven for 5 minutes. Remove from the oven, turn the skewers and cook and additional 5 minutes. The high heat of the oven should give the kebabs a nice sear.

9. Serve with the lemon wedges.

Nutritional Info: Calories: 667, Sodium: 486mg, Dietary Fiber: 1.4 g, Total Fat: 27.7 g, Total Carbs: 6.6 g, Protein: 92.8 g.

Sous Vide Tandoori Lamb Chops

Servings: 8 | Prep time: 2 1/2 hours | Cook time: 2-3 hours

For a fun twist on traditional lamb chops, try this Indian inspired rub for delicious results. Garam Masala is the base for many popular Indian dishes like Chicken Tikka Masala and will give your meat dishes an amazing burst of deep flavor.

Ingredients:

8 lamb rib chops (2 1/2 pounds)

3/4 cups Greek yogurt

1/4 cup heavy cream

3 tablespoons fresh lemon juice

1 (3-inch piece) fresh ginger, peeled and minced

4 large garlic cloves, minced

1 tablespoon malt vinegar

1 tablespoon garam masala

1 tablespoon ground cumin

1 tablespoon paprika

1/2 teaspoon cayenne pepper

Salt

Instructions:

1. Set your Anova to 135F/57.2C.
2. In a large bowl, whisk the yogurt with the heavy cream, lemon juice, ginger, garlic, malt vinegar, garam masala, cumin, paprika, cayenne, and 1 teaspoon of salt.
3. Place lamb chops in a large vacuum-sealed bag or place two to three chops in smaller bags.
4. Pour the yogurt marinade over the lamb and seal using your vacuum-sealed.

5.   Place the bag in the refrigerator to marinate for 2 hours.

6.   When your water bath is ready, submerge the bag and cook for at least 2 hours and not more than 3 hours.

7.   When the lamb is almost finished, heat your oven to 450F.

8.   Remove the lamb from the bag and transfer to a baking sheet. Cook in the oven for 6 minutes, and turn the chops over. Cook an additional 6 minutes and serve.

Nutritional Info: Calories: 308, Sodium: 122 mg, Dietary Fiber: 0.6 g, Total Fat: 12.7 g, Total Carbs: 3.1 g, Protein: 42.9 g.

Sous Vide Shawarma Leg of Lamb

Servings: 6 | Prep time: 10 minutes | Cook time: 14 hours

This Middle Eastern flavored lamb shank cooks low and slow to perfection. The blend of exotic spices is the perfect complement to this traditional Middle Eastern favorite.

Ingredients:

1 (5-pound) bone-in leg of lamb,

Salt, freshly ground pepper

2 tablespoons cumin seeds

2 teaspoons caraway seeds

2 teaspoons coriander seeds

2 Thai chilies, very finely chopped

4 garlic cloves, finely grated

1/2 cup olive oil

1 tablespoon paprika

1/2 teaspoon ground cinnamon

Instructions:

1. Set your Anova to 143F/62C.

2. In a large bowl combine, salt, pepper, cumin, caraway, coriander, chilies, garlic, olive oil, paprika, and cinnamon.

3. Rub the mixture all over the lamb and place in a vacuum-sealed bag.

4. Seal the bag with your Foodsaver or any vacuum sealer available and place in the refrigerator for 2 hours.

5. Submerge the lamb in the water bath and cook for 12 hours. For an even more tender texture cook an additional 6 hours.

Nutritional Info: Calories: 864, Sodium: 319 mg, Dietary Fiber: 1.1 g, Total Fat: 45.2 g, Total Carbs: 2.8 g, Protein: 107 g.

Sous Vide Herbed Lamb Chops

Servings: 6 | Prep time: 1 hour | Cook time: 2-4 hours

This is a simple and flavorful way of preparing lamb chops with just a hint of heat.

Ingredients:

4 large garlic cloves, pressed

1 tablespoon fresh thyme leaves, lightly crushed

1 tablespoon fresh rosemary leaves, lightly crushed

1 teaspoon cayenne pepper

2 teaspoons coarse salt

2 tablespoons extra-virgin olive oil, divided

6 (1 1/4-inch thick) lamb loin chops

Instructions:

1. Set your Anova to 135F/57.2C

2. In a vacuum-sealed bag combine the herbs, cayenne pepper, salt, pepper, oil, and lamb chops.

3. Seal the bag and allow to marinate in the refrigerator for 1 hour.

4. Submerge in the water bath and cook for at least 2 hours and not more than 4 hours. When chops are almost finished, heat a skillet over high heat.

5. Remove chops from the bag and sear for 3 minutes per side before serving.

6. These chops pair well with a roasted garlic mashed potato.

Nutritional Info: Calories: 205, Sodium: 841 mg, Dietary Fiber: 0.5 g, Total Fat: 11.1g, Total Carbs: 1.5 g, Protein: 24.1 g.

Sous Vide Lamb Casserole

Servings: 6 | Prep time: 20 minutes | Cook time: 2-4 hours

This is an old fashioned treat that's great for warming up on cold days. And since you're not cooking in the oven, you don't have to constantly keep an eye on your diner.

Ingredients:

2 tablespoons flour

salt and pepper

1 1/2 pounds lamb neck fillet, diced

2 tablespoons vegetable oil

1 medium onion

1 carrot, peeled and diced

1 teaspoon ground cinnamon

28 ounces chopped tomatoes

2 teaspoons honey

2 cups chicken or lamb stock

1/2 pound small red potatoes

1 package frozen peas

Instructions:

1. Set your Anova to 180F/82.2C.

2. Combine the salt, pepper, and flour and toss the lamb pieces to coat. Then, in a medium skillet heat the oil.

3. Brown the lamb on all sides and remove from heat.

4. Add the onion and carrots to the pan and cook for 5 minutes, until lightly browned. Toss in the cinnamon.

5. Transfer the lamb, vegetables, and all remaining ingredients to a vacuum-sealed bag.

6. Submerge the bag in the water bath and cook for at least 2 and not more than 4 hours.

7. Remove the bag from the water and pour contents into a casserole dish. The liquid in the bag should have thickened into a nice smooth gravy.

Nutritional Info: Calories: 434, Sodium: 163 mg, Dietary Fiber: 5.5 g, Total Fat: 14.7 g, Total Carbs: 24.1 g, Protein: 50 g.

Sous Vide Lamb Loin with Cherry-Balsamic Sauce

Servings: 2 | Prep time: 10 minutes | Cook time: 2-4 hours

This tender, juicy lamb loin goes well with a rich cherry sauce that you can make in your sous vide as well.

Ingredients:

1 (1-pound) boneless lamb loin roast

salt and freshly ground black pepper

1 tablespoon chopped plus 2 whole sprigs fresh rosemary

2 tablespoons unsalted butter

1 medium red onion, thinly sliced

1/2 pound fresh cherries, pitted and chopped

1/4 cup balsamic vinegar

Instructions:

1. Set your Anova to 134F/57C.

2. Season the lamb with salt, pepper and one sprig of rosemary, seal in a vacuum-sealed bag and submerge in the water bath for at least 2 hours and not more than 4.

3. While the lamb cooks, combine the butter, onion, cherries, and vinegar in another vacuum-sealed bag.

4. An hour before the lamb has finished, add the sauce bag to the water bath and cook until the lamb is done.

5. Remove both bags from the water bath.

6. Slice the lamb into 3/4-inch-thick pieces and top with sauce.

Nutritional Info: Calories: 691, Sodium: 280 mg, Dietary Fiber: 3.0 g, Total Fat: 28.7 g, Total Carbs: 38.9 g, Protein: 65.0 g.

Simple Sous Vide Rack of Lamb

Servings: 2 | Prep time: 1 hour | Cook time: 2-4 hours

Cooking a whole rack of lamb can be tricky, but your sous vide removes all the guess work. And because the Foodsaver does such an excellent job of creating a vacuum seal, your lamb rack will be cooked to even perfection.

Ingredients:

2 racks of lamb, trimmed

1 clove garlic, minced

2 teaspoons salt

1/3 cup fresh rosemary leaves

1/2 teaspoon freshly ground black pepper

2 teaspoons extra-virgin olive oil

Instructions:

1. Set your Anova to 134F/56.5C.
2. Combine the garlic, salt, rosemary leaves, and pepper, and rub all over the racks.
3. Place the racks into separate vacuum-sealed bags. Marinate the bags in the refrigerator for 1 hour before submerging in the water bath.
4. Cook the racks in the water bath for between 2 to 4 hours.
5. When the lamb is almost done, heat your oven to 450F.
6. Remove the racks from the vacuum-sealed bags and place on a baking sheet or roasting pan.
7. Roast in the oven for about 10 minutes.
   Remove from the oven and serve immediately.

Nutritional Info: Calories: 224, Sodium: 2392 mg, Dietary Fiber: 4.3 g, Total Fat: 12 g, Total Carbs: 7 g, Protein: 23.1 g.

Sous Vide Slow Cooked Lamb Shanks

Servings: 4 | Prep time: 10 minutes | Cook time: 48 hours

One of the biggest advantages of sous vide cooking is that you can cook without constantly checking on your food. These lamb shanks cook at an even temperature to produce perfect fall off the bone meat.

Ingredients:

2 bone-in lamb shanks

Salt and black pepper

6 sprigs fresh thyme

2 cloves garlic, crushed

Instructions:

1. Set your Anova for 143F/62C.

2. Rub the lamb shanks all over with the salt and pepper and place into separate vacuum-sealed bags.

3. Add three sprigs of thyme and one clove of crushed garlic to each bag.

4. Seal the bags and submerge in the water bath for 48 hours.

5. When the lamb is nearly finished in the water bath, heat your oven to 500F.

6. Remove the lamb from the bags and place on a baking sheet or roasting pan.

7. Cook in the oven for 10 minutes to achieve a nice sear.

8. At this point the lamb should be crispy on the outside and fall-off-the-bone tender on the inside.

Nutritional Info: Calories: 319, Sodium: 127mg, Dietary Fiber: 1.7 g, Total Fat: 12.3 g, Total Carbs: 3.4 g, Protein: 46.4 g.

Sous Vide Slow Cooked Lamb Shoulder

Servings: 4 Prep time: 10 minutes | Cook time: 8 hours

This cut of lamb can be tricky because if it isn't cooked long enough it can turn out tough but the even heat from your sous vide will ensure that it is fall off the bone tender.

Ingredients:

1 whole lamb shoulder, deboned

Salt and pepper

3 tablespoons olive oil

1 clove of garlic, crushed

Large sprig for each thyme, rosemary and mint

Instructions:

1. Set your Anova to 182F/83.3 C.
2. Rub the lamb with salt and pepper, and place inside a vacuum-sealed bag. Add the garlic, oil, and herbs.
3. Seal the bag and submerge in the water bath for 8 hours.
4. When the lamb is almost finished cooking, heat your broiler to high.
5. Remove the lamb from the water bath and place on a baking sheet, fat side up.
6. Broil for 8 to 10 minutes or until the fat side is crispy.

Nutritional Info: Calories: 329, Sodium: 96 mg, Dietary Fiber: 0.7 g, Total Fat: 19.9 g, Total Carbs: 1.3 g, Protein: 35.3 g.

Sous Vide Rosemary Lamb Chops

Servings: 2 | Prep time: 10 minutes | Cook time: 2 hours

Lamb chops are a savory treat, but cooking them sous vide will lock in all of their rich flavor. This recipe shows you how to use herbs to elevate lamb chops while still retaining their complex character.

Ingredients:

1 1/2 teaspoons chopped fresh rosemary

1/2 teaspoon salt

1/4 teaspoon freshly ground black pepper

1 garlic clove, minced

8 (3-ounce) lamb rib chops, trimmed

2 teaspoons olive oil

Instructions:

1. Set your Anova to 140F/60C.
2. Place the lamb chops in a vacuum-sealed bag with the rosemary, salt, and pepper, and seal.
3. Submerge in the water bath, and cook for 2 hours.
4. When the lamb is almost finished, heat a skillet over medium heat, and brown the garlic.
5. Add the lamb and cook until the chops have browned.
6. Remove from heat and serve immediately.

Nutritional Info: Calories: 679, Sodium: 841 mg, Dietary Fiber: 0 g, Total Fat: 29.8 g, Total Carbs: 1.2 g, Protein: 95.7 g.

13

PORK

Sous Vide Carolina Pulled Pork

Servings: 6-8 | Prep time: 20 minutes | Cook time: 24 hours

This traditional barbecue favorite stands out because of its punchy, tangy sauce.

Ingredients:

For the pork:

- 1 (2-3 pounds) pork shoulder
- 1 teaspoon mild paprika
- 2 teaspoons light brown sugar
- 1 1/2 teaspoons hot paprika
- 1/2 teaspoon celery salt
- 1/2 teaspoon garlic salt
- 1/2 teaspoon dry mustard
- 1/2 teaspoon freshly ground black pepper
- 1/2 teaspoon onion powder
- 1/4 teaspoon salt

For the Sauce:

- 1 1/2 cups yellow mustard
- 1/2 cup brown sugar
- 3/4 cups cider vinegar
- 3/4 cups beer
- 1 teaspoon fresh ground pepper
- 1/2 teaspoon cayenne pepper
- 1 1/2 teaspoons Worcestershire sauce
- 2 tablespoons butter, melted
- 1 1/2 teaspoons liquid smoke

Instructions:

1. Set your Anova to 140F/60C.
2. Combine all the spices for the pork in a small bowl and rub the mixture all over the pork shoulder.
3. Place the pork shoulder in a vacuum-sealed bag.
4. Submerge the bag in the water and cook for 24 hours.
5. To make the sauce, combine all sauce ingredients in a medium saucepan and heat over low heat until just bubbling.
6. Remove the pork from the water bath and place in a large bowl.
7. Pour in the sauce, and with two forks, shred the pork and mix with the sauce.
8. Serve on soft buns and top with your favorite coleslaw.

Nutritional Info: Calories: 603, Sodium: 757 mg, Dietary Fiber: 2.0 g, Total Fat: 41.3 g, Total Carbs: 13.6 g, Protein: 41.9 g.

Sous Vide Barbecue Pork Ribs

Servings: 4 | Prep time: 20 minutes | Cook time: 12 hours

Barbecue ribs are a perennial favorite, and this recipe will show you how to make perfect ribs without a smoker. Of course a great rub is the key to great ribs.

Ingredients:

2 racks of St. Louis or baby back ribs

1 teaspoon liquid hickory smoke

1/3 cup paprika

1/3 cup dark brown sugar

1/4 cup salt

2 tablespoons whole yellow mustard seed

1 teaspoon freshly ground black pepper

2 teaspoons granulated garlic powder

1 tablespoon dried oregano

Instructions:

1. Set your Anova to 165F/74C.
2. Combine the paprika, sugar, salt, mustard seed, pepper, garlic powder, and oregano.
3. Remove the silver skin on the back of the ribs and cut into three or four rib sections.
4. Coat the ribs in the spice mix and place in a vacuum-sealed bags.
5. Place in the water bath and cook for 12 hours.
6. Remove from the water bath and pat dry with paper towels.
7. Heat your oven to 300F and coat the racks with your favorite barbecue sauce.

8.   Cook ribs in the oven for about 30-40 minutes. A nice coating of sauce will form.

9.   Note: Feel free to add more sauce while the ribs are in the oven for even more flavor.

Nutritional Info: Calories: 326, Sodium: 77 mg, Dietary Fiber: 4.7 g, Total Fat: 14.9 g, Total Carbs: 20.6 g, Protein: 29.0 g.

Sous Vide Adobo Pork Ribs

Servings: 4 | Prep time: 20 minutes | Cook time: 12 hours

These tender ribs are enhanced with traditional adobo seasonings for a punch of flavor that is both tangy and spicy.

Ingredients:

1 cup apple cider vinegar

1 tablespoon soy sauce

3 bay leaves

1 large jalapeño chili, chopped

1 side baby-back pork ribs, cut into individual ribs

2 teaspoons sea salt

6 garlic cloves, peeled

2 teaspoons black peppercorns

Instructions:

1. Set your Anova to 165F/74C.

2. In a bowl, combine the vinegar, soy sauce, bay leaves, and chilies.

3. Season the ribs with salt and place inside a vacuum-sealed bag with the garlic, pepper, and vinegar mixture. Seal the bag and submerge in the water bath for 12 hours.

4. When the ribs are nearly finished in the water bath, preheat your oven to 400F.

5. Remove the ribs from the bag and pour 1/4 cup of the liquid over the ribs. Place in the oven for 10-15 minutes, or until browned.

6. Serve with steamed rice and the remaining cooking liquid.

Nutritional Info: Calories: 520, Sodium: 1381 mg, Dietary Fiber: 1.0 g, Total Fat: 12.3 g, Total Carbs: 1.0 g, Protein: 90.0 g.

Sous Vide Spicy Korean Pork Ribs

Servings: 4 | Prep time: 10 minutes | Cook time: 12 hours

These Korean style ribs pack a punch thanks to a hot pepper paste known as gochujang. Your Foodsaver will lock in the flavor by creating a perfect vacuum seal.

Ingredients:

3 pounds baby back pork ribs, separated into individual ribs

1/2 cup gochujang

2 tablespoons dark brown sugar

2 tablespoons soy sauce

2 tablespoons rice vinegar

2 teaspoons toasted sesame oil

Salt to taste

Instructions:

1. Set your Anova to 165F/74C.

2. In a bowl, combine the gochujang, brown sugar, soy sauce, vinegar, and sesame oil.

3. Season the ribs with salt and place in a vacuum-sealed bag. Add the marinade to the bag and seal.

4. Submerge the bag in the water bath and cook for 12 hours.

5. When the ribs are nearly finished, heat your oven to 450F. Remove the ribs from the bag and reserve the marinade. Place the ribs on a baking sheet and brush with the reserved marinade.

6. Cook in the oven for 15 minutes and baste again with marinade. Cook an additional 10 minutes.

Nutritional Info: Calories: 536, Sodium: 1407 mg, Dietary Fiber: 0 g, Total Fat: 14.3 g, Total Carbs: 5.5 g, Protein: 89.7 g.

Sous Vide Rosemary Lamb Chops

Servings: 2 | Prep time: 10 minutes | Cook time: 2 hours

Lamb chops are a savory treat, but cooking them sous vide will lock in all of their rich flavor. This recipe shows you how to use herbs to elevate lamb chops while still retaining their complex character.

Ingredients:

8 (3-ounce) lamb rib chops, trimmed

1 1/2 teaspoons chopped fresh rosemary

1/2 teaspoon salt

1/4 teaspoon freshly ground black pepper

1 garlic clove, minced

2 teaspoons olive oil

Instructions:

1. Set your Anova to 140F/60C.

2. Place the lamb chops in a vacuum-sealed bag with the rosemary, salt, and pepper, and seal.

3. Submerge in the water bath, and cook for 2 hours.

4. When the lamb is almost finished, heat a skillet over medium heat, and brown the garlic.

5. Add the lamb and cook until the chops have browned.

6. Remove from heat and serve immediately.

Nutritional Info: Calories: 679, Sodium: 841 mg, Dietary Fiber: 0 g, Total Fat: 29.8 g, Total Carbs: 1.2 g, Protein: 95.7 g.

Sous Vide Herbed Pork Chops

Servings: 4 | Prep time: 10 minutes | Cook time: 1 hour

These chops are full of flavor, and thanks to your Anova, they're guaranteed to come out perfectly every time.

Ingredients:

4 bone-in pork chops

4 sprigs fresh rosemary

2 cloves garlic, crushed

2 tablespoons olive oil

2 tablespoons butter

Salt and pepper

Instructions:

1. Heat your Anova to 140F/60C for medium rare chops. For medium well, set your Anova to 150F/66C.

2. Place the chops, herbs, salt, pepper, and butter in a vacuum-sealed bag.

3. Submerge in the water bath for at least 1 hour and not more than 4.

4. When the chops are nearly finished, heat a skillet (preferably cast iron) on high heat with the olive oil.

5. Remove chops from the bag and sear quickly on both side until a nice crust is achieved.

6. Remove from the pan and serve immediately.

Nutritional Info: Calories: 370, Sodium: 97 mg, Dietary Fiber: 0 g, Total Fat: 32.5 g, Total Carbs: 0.6 g, Protein: 18.2 g.

Sous Vide Cochinita Pibil

Servings: 6 | Prep time: 15 minutes | Cook time: 12-24 hours

Cochinita Pibil is a Mayan style pit pork that is cooked low and slow to tender perfection.

Ingredients:

1 boneless pork shoulder

3/4 cups crumbled achiote paste

3 tablespoons orange juice

1 tablespoon white wine vinegar

2 garlic cloves, minced

1/4 teaspoons dried oregano

3 medium yellow onions, quartered

1/2 cup water

Instructions:

1. Set your Anova to 158F/70C.

2. Combine the achiote paste, orange juice, vinegar, garlic, and oregano in a bowl and mix well.

3. Season the pork shoulder with the mixture so that it is fully coated.

4. Place the pork in a vacuum-sealed bag with the quartered onions, water, and remaining seasoning mixture.

5. Seal the bag and submerge in the water bath for 12 to 24 hours.

6. Remove the pork from the water bath, pour entire contents into a large bowl.

7. Using forks, shred the pork and onions, and mix with the cooking liquid. The pork should be so tender that it falls apart easily.

8.   Serve with salsa and corn tortillas.

Nutritional Info: Calories: 405, Sodium: 776 mg, Dietary Fiber: 1.2 g, Total Fat: 34.6 g, Total Carbs: 6.3 g, Protein: 97.9 g.

Sous Vide Herbed Pork Roast

Servings: 6 | Prep time: 10 minutes | Cook time: 2-4 hours

Pork roast is a traditional favorite, but even cooking can be difficult. Thanks to your Anova, you can have perfectly cooked roasts every time.

Ingredients:

1 (5 pound) boneless pork loin

1 teaspoon rubbed sage

1/2 teaspoon salt

1/4 teaspoon pepper

1 clove garlic, crushed

1/2 cup sugar

1 tablespoon cornstarch

1/4 cup vinegar

1/4 cup water

2 tablespoons soy sauce

Instructions:

1. Set your Anova to 140F/60C.
2. In a bowl, combine the sage, salt, pepper, and garlic.
3. Rub the mixture liberally on the pork and place in a vacuum-sealed bag.
4. Submerge the bag in the water bath and cook for at least 2 hours and not more than 4.
5. When the pork is nearly finished, heat your oven to 450F.
6. In a saucepan, combine the sugar, cornstarch, vinegar, water, and soy sauce.
7. Cook over medium heat until the sauce has reduced and slightly thickened.
8. Remove the pork from the water bath and place on a baking sheet or roasting pan.
9. Baste with the mixture and place in the oven for 20 minutes.

10.   Remove roast from the oven and slice into 1/2-inch-thick pieces.

Nutritional Info: Calories: 989, Sodium: 730 mg, Dietary Fiber: 0 g, Total Fat: 52.6 g, Total Carbs: 18.7 g, Protein: 103.6 g.

Sous Vide Espresso-Chili Ribs

Servings: 6 | Prep time: 10 minutes | Cook time: 12 hours

Espresso isn't just for drinking. As this recipe will demonstrate, it can make for a deeply flavorful addition to a traditional spice rub.

Ingredients:

4 pounds baby back pork ribs

2 tablespoons cayenne pepper

1 tablespoon paprika

1 tablespoon ground cumin

1 1/2 teaspoons salt

3/4 teaspoons ground black pepper

1 (12-ounce) bottle dark beer

Your favorite barbecue sauce

1/2 cup water

2 tablespoons light brown sugar

1 tablespoon instant espresso powder

Instructions:

1. Set your Anova to 165F/74C.

2. In a small bowl, combine the cayenne pepper, paprika, cumin, salt, and pepper.

3. Rub the spice mix on the ribs, covering completely.

4. Place the ribs in a vacuum-sealed bag but don't seal it just yet.

5. In a small saucepan, reduce the beer by about half and pour into the bag with the ribs and then seal.

6. Submerge the bag in the water bath and cook for 12 hours.

7.   When the ribs are nearly finished cooking, combine the barbecue sauce, water, brown sugar, and espresso powder in a medium saucepan over low heat.

8.   Remove the ribs from the water bath and pat dry with paper towels.

9.   Heat your oven to 400F and brush the barbecue sauce mixture over the ribs.

10.   Place the ribs on a baking sheet and cook in the oven for 10 minutes.

11.   Brush another coating of sauce onto the ribs and cook an additional 10 minutes.

Note: Serve ribs with the remaining barbecue sauce on the side.

Nutritional Info: Calories: 482, Sodium: 760 mg, Dietary Fiber: 1.1 g, Total Fat: 11.3 g, Total Carbs: 7.2 g, Protein: 80 g.

Sous Vide Pork Medallions with Fennel

Servings: 6 | Prep time: 10 minutes | Cook time: 2 hours

Fennel cooked low and slow in the sous vide can unlock its complex flavors. And it can be cooked at the same time as the pork medallions.

Ingredients:

1 1/2 pounds pork loin, cut into medallions

Salt & ground pepper

4 tablespoons olive oil, plus more for serving

2 fennel bulbs, trimmed and thinly sliced

Juice of 1/2 lemon

1 sprig fresh thyme

1 spring fresh oregano

2 cloves garlic, peeled and lightly crushed

Chopped fresh parsley, for serving

Instructions:

1. Set your Anova to 140F/60C.
2. Rub the pork with salt and pepper, and 1 tablespoon of oil, and place in one vacuum-sealed bag.
3. In another vacuum-sealed bag, combine 1 tablespoon of oil, fennel, lemon juice, thyme, oregano, and garlic. Submerge both bags in the water bath and cook for 2 hours.
4. Just before removing the bags from the water bath, heat a large skillet on medium heat and add the remaining oil.
5. Place the pork medallions and the fennel mixture in the pan and cook the pork for 2 minutes per side.
6. Remove from heat and garnish with fresh parsley.

Nutritional Info: Calories: 385, Sodium: 112 mg, Dietary Fiber: 3.0 g, Total Fat: 25.4 g, Total Carbs: 7.2 g, Protein: 32.2 g.

Sous Vide Indian Spiced Pork Meatballs

Servings: 8 | Prep time: 15 minutes | Cook time: 1 hour

Cooking meatballs sous vide ensures rich flavor as well as guaranteed tenderness.

Ingredients:

1 pound ground pork

1 egg, lightly beaten

1/3 cup bread crumbs

1 red chili, seeded and finely chopped

2 teaspoons grated fresh ginger

1 onion, grated

1 teaspoon garam masala

2 tablespoons chopped fresh cilantro

Sea salt & ground pepper

1 tablespoon vegetable oil

Instructions:

1. Set your Anova to 140F/60C.

2. In a large bowl, combine pork, onion, egg, bread crumbs, chili, ginger, garam masala, cilantro, salt, and pepper and mix well.

3. Using a spoon, shape the mixture into small balls and place inside a vacuum-sealed bag.

4. Seal the bag and submerge in the water bath, cooking for at least 1 hour and not more than 3.

5. When the meatballs are nearly finished, heat a large skillet over high heat and add the oil.

6. Remove the meatballs from the bag and place in the skillet, cooking until they are just browned.

7. Remove and serve immediately.

Nutritional Info: Calories: 130, Sodium: 106 mg, Dietary Fiber: 0.6 g, Total Fat: 4.5 g, Total Carbs: 5.1 g, Protein: 16.4 g.

Sous Vide Five Spice Pork Tenderloin

Servings: 6 | Prep time: 10 minutes | Cook time: 2 hours

This recipe uses a traditional Chinese spice blend to add deep, rich flavor to a pork tenderloin.

Ingredients:

1 1/2 pounds pork tenderloin

1 tablespoon five-spice powder

1 teaspoon dry mustard

1/2 teaspoon ground ginger

1/2 teaspoon pepper

1/2 teaspoon salt

2 tablespoons peanut oil

1/3 cup hoisin sauce

Instructions:

1. Set your Anova to 140F/60C.
2. In a small bowl, combine the five spice powder, mustard, ginger, salt, and pepper.
3. Rub the spice mix on the pork loin and seal in a vacuum-sealed bag. Submerge the bag and cook for 2 hours.
4. When the pork is nearly finished, heat your oven to 450F.
5. Remove the pork from the bag and place on a baking sheet.
6. Roast in the oven for 10 minutes, or just enough time for the outside to brown slightly.
7. Remove from the oven, slice, and serve with hoisin sauce.

Nutritional Info: Calories: 241, Sodium: 488 mg, Dietary Fiber: 1.1 g, Total Fat: 9.1 g, Total Carbs: 7.0 g, Protein: 30.6 g.

Simple Sous Vide Pork Belly

Servings: 4 | Prep time: 10 minutes | Cook time: 7-8 hours

Sous vide is the best method for perfectly cooked pork belly, and this recipe will show you the secrets of adding even more flavor courtesy of your Foodsaver and the right seasonings.

Ingredients:

1 pound pork belly	*1/4 cup soy sauce*
1 clove garlic, crushed	*Salt*
3/4 cups dry white wine	*Black pepper*

Instructions:

1. Set your Anova at 176F/80C.
2. Combine all ingredients in a vacuum-sealed bag.
3. Submerge bag in water bath and cook for 7 to 8 hours.
4. Remove the bag and reserve the liquid from the bag.
5. Pour the liquid in a saucepan and reduce by about half until the liquid has thickened.
6. Glaze the pork belly with the sauce, slice, and serve.

Nutritional Info: Calories: 550, Sodium: 2732 mg, Dietary Fiber: 0 g, Total Fat: 30.6 g, Total Carbs: 2.1 g, Protein: 53.4 g.

14

BEEF

The Ultimate Sous Vide Meatloaf

Servings: 6 | Prep time: 30 minutes | Cook time: 2 hours

This isn't just a meatloaf recipe, it's quite possibly the most flavorful meatloaf recipe ever, and thanks to your Anova, it will be cooked to perfection.

Ingredients:

2 tablespoons olive oil

1/2 yellow onion, peeled and diced

1/4 yellow bell pepper, seeded and diced

1/4 green bell pepper, seeded and diced

1/4 red bell pepper, seeded and diced

1/2 cup tomato, pureed

2 large eggs

1/4 cup heavy cream

1 tablespoons Worcestershire sauce

1 teaspoons sea salt

1/2 teaspoon ground black pepper

1/2 teaspoon paprika

1/4 teaspoon garlic powder

1/2 pound ground sirloin

1/2 ground pork

1/4 sweet Italian sausage

Instructions:

1. Set your Anova to 140F/60C.
2. In a medium saucepan, heat the olive oil over medium heat, and add the onions, peppers, and tomato.
3. Cook until peppers and onions are soft.
4. In a large bowl, combine the eggs, cream, onions and peppers, and all of the seasonings.
5. Finally, add the ground meat and stir until it is well combined.

6. Pour mixture into a large vacuum-sealed bag.

7. Seal the bag so that a basic loaf shape is maintained at the bottom, and submerge it in the water bath for at least 2, but not more than 6 hours.

8. When the meatloaf is nearly finished, heat your broiler to high.

9. Remove the meatloaf from the bag and place on a baking sheet or roasting pan.

10. Broil for 5 minutes and flip.

11. Broil for another 5 minutes and remove from the broiler.

Nutritional Info: Calories: 299, Sodium: 660 mg, Dietary Fiber: 0.8 g, Total Fat: 16.1 g, Total Carbs: 4.3 g, Protein: 33.4 g.

Sous Vide Spice Rubbed Filet Mignon

Servings: 4 | Prep time: 10 minutes | Cook time: 45 minutes

Filet is a luxurious cut but without some extra flavor it can be a bit dull. Usually filet is accompanied by a rich sauce, but a spice rub is even better for coaxing out the delicate flavor of the meat.

Ingredients:

4 thick cut filets

2 tablespoons paprika

2 tablespoons ground cumin

2 tablespoons dry mustard

1 tablespoon black pepper

2 tablespoons salt

2 tablespoons butter

Instructions:

1. Set your Anova to 135F/57.2C for medium or 125F/51.6C for medium rare.
2. In a bowl, combine the paprika, cumin, mustard, salt, & pepper.
3. Rub the filets with the spice blend and place in individual vacuum-sealed bags.
4. Submerge the bags in the water bath and cook for at least 45 minutes and not more than 2 hours.
5. When the filets are finished in the water bath, heat a large cast iron pan over high heat.
6. Sear the filets for 2 minutes per side and then add the butter, and cook for an additional 2 minutes. Remove from the pan and serve immediately.

Nutritional Info: Calories: 260, Sodium: 2912 mg, Dietary Fiber: 0 g, Total Fat: 13.8 g, Total Carbs: 6.2 g, Protein: 28.5 g.

Sous Vide Keema

Servings: 6 | Prep time: 20 minutes | Cook time: 45 minutes

This Pakistani ground beef casserole features subtle spices that create an adventurous dining experience that can be prepared in less than an hour using your Anova.

Ingredients:

1 1/2 pounds lean ground sirloin

1 cup chopped onions

2 cups canned crushed tomatoes

1 cup frozen peas

1 cup diced potatoes

1/2 teaspoon each cinnamon, turmeric, ginger

1 tablespoon curry powder

Salt

Ground black pepper

Instructions:

1. Set your Anova to 140F/65C.
2. In a large skillet, brown the meat and add the onions, cooking until the beef is browned.
3. Place the beef and onions in a vacuum-sealed bag and add the tomatoes, peas, potatoes, spices.
4. Seal the bag and submerge in the water bath for 45 minutes.
5. Remove the bag from the water, season with salt and pepper and serve over rice.

Nutritional Info: Calories: 149, Sodium: 206 mg, Dietary Fiber: 5.7 g, Total Fat: 4.4 g, Total Carbs: 17.3 g, Protein: 10.7 g.

Sous Vide Chili Con Carne

Servings: 8 | Prep time: 20 minutes | Cook time: 12 hours

This is quite possibly the easiest chili recipe of all time, and because your Anova keeps everything at an even temperature, you don't even have to check on it.

Ingredients:

1 tablespoon oil

1 large onion

1 red pepper, sliced

2 garlic cloves, peeled

1 teaspoon hot cayenne pepper

1 tablespoon mild chili powder

1 teaspoon paprika

1 teaspoon ground cumin

1 pound lean ground beef

1 cup beef stock or broth

3/4 pounds chopped tomatoes

1 teaspoon sugar

2 tablespoons tomato purée

3/4 pounds red kidney beans

Instructions:

1. 1. Set your Anova to 170F/76C.
2. In a large skillet heat the oil and add the garlic, onion and red pepper, cooking until they become transparent. Add the cayenne pepper, chili powder, paprika, cumin, and beef broth.
3. Simmer for 5 minutes and pour into a large vacuum-sealed bag.
4. In the same pan, brown the beef and add the tomatoes.
5. Add the beef mixture to the vacuum-sealed bag along with the sugar, tomato puree, and beans.
6. Seal the bag and submerge in the water bath for 12 hours.

7. Remove the bag from the water and serve chili over rice.

Nutritional Info: Calories: 294, Sodium: 154 mg, Dietary Fiber: 8.2 g, Total Fat: 6.2 g, Total Carbs: 32.1 g, Protein: 28.2 g.

Sous Vide Mongolian Beef

Servings: 4 | Prep time: 20 minutes | Cook time: 1 hour

A favorite at Chinese restaurants, this Mongolian beef is made even more tender and flavorful with the even temperature provided by your Anova. And since your Foodsaver promises to seal perfectly every time, you can cook the beef in the rich sauce.

Ingredients:

2 teaspoons vegetable oil

1/2 teaspoon minced ginger

1 tablespoon chopped garlic

1/2 cup soy sauce

1/2 cup water

3/4 cups dark brown sugar

1 pound flank steak

1/4 cup cornstarch

2 green onions, sliced

Instructions:

1. Set your Anova to 140F/65C

2. Heat a pan over medium heat and add the garlic, ginger, soy sauce, and water. Let simmer for a moment and then add the brown sugar. Stir until the sauce thickens slightly.

3. Slice the steak into strips and place in a vacuum-sealed bag.

4. Pour the sauce into the bag with the beef and seal.

5. Submerge in the water bath and cook for 1 hour.

6. Remove from water bath and serve with sliced green onion and steamed rice.

Nutritional Info: Calories: 397, Sodium: 1871 mg, Dietary Fiber: 0.6 g, Total Fat: 11.7 g, Total Carbs: 37.8 g, Protein: 33.9 g.

Sous Vide Corned Beef

Servings: 6 | Prep time: 30 minutes | Cook time: 48 hours

This traditional Irish favorite is easy to make in your Anova, and the long cooking time will ensure deep rich flavor.

Ingredients:

1 (5-pound) beef brisket

1 cup dark beer

1 cup beef stock

2 tablespoons pickling spice

1 onion, sliced

1 head cabbage (optional)

Instructions:

1. Set your Anova to 135F/57.2C.
2. Rub the brisket with pickling spice and place in a vacuum-sealed bag with the beer, beef stock, and onion.
3. Seal the bag and submerge in the water bath for 48 hours.
4. Remove from the water bath and slice against the grain.
5. Bonus: If you want to accompany your corned beef with braised cabbage, remove the brisket from the bag and replace with chopped cabbage. Mix with the cooking liquid and use your Foodsaver to reseal the bag. Submerge in the water bath for 30 minutes and serve.

Nutritional Info: Calories: 759, Sodium: 403 mg, Dietary Fiber: 3.5 g, Total Fat: 23.8 g, Total Carbs: 10.0 g, Protein: 117.0 g.

Sous Vide Beef Stroganoff

Servings: 6 | Prep time: 20 minutes | Cook time: 1 hour

This traditional favorite can be made sous vide for even more tender beef, and since this recipe uses less oil than most recipes, it is also a healthier option.

Ingredients:

1 1/2 pounds sirloin steak, cut into strips

2 cups sliced white or Cremini mushrooms

2 onions, sliced

1 clove garlic, chopped

2 tablespoons butter

1/2 teaspoon salt

1 1/2 cups low sodium beef broth

1 teaspoon Worcestershire sauce

1/4 cup flour

1 cup fat free sour cream

3 cups cooked egg noodles

Instructions:

1. Set your Anova to 150F/65.5C.
2. In a medium skillet cook the onions and mushrooms until onions become transparent and remove from heat.
3. Place beef in a vacuum-sealed bag with the broth, onion mixture, Worcestershire sauce, flour, and sour cream. Seal the bag and submerge in the water bath for 1 hour.
4. While the beef cooks, bring a pot of salted water to a boil, and add the noodles.
5. When the beef has finished cooking, remove from bag and mix with the noodles. The sauce should be creamy.

Nutritional Info: Calories: 445, Sodium: 536 mg, Dietary Fiber: 2.1 g, Total Fat: 13.1 g, Total Carbs: 35.5 g, Protein: 42.3 g.

Sous Vide Marinated T-Bone Steaks

Servings: 4 | Prep time: 10 minutes | Cook time: 1 hour

A great marinade can be the secret to a legendary steak. This recipe will take any cut of beef to a new level of flavor.

Ingredients:

4 T- bone steaks

2 cups vegetable oil

1 cup soy sauce

1 cup Worcestershire sauce

1/2 cup pineapple juice

2 tablespoons granulated garlic

2 tablespoons freshly ground black pepper

2 tablespoons dry mustard

Instructions:

1. Combine the oil, soy sauce, Worcestershire sauce, pineapple juice, garlic, pepper, and mustard in a bowl, and refrigerate for 6 hours.

2. Place each steak in a vacuum-sealed bag and pour in some of the marinade. Seal the bags and place in the refrigerator for one hour.

3. Set your Anova to 125F/51.6C for medium rare or 135F/57.2C for medium steaks.

4. Submerge the bags in the water bath and cook for at least 1 hour and not more than 3 hours.

5. When the steaks are nearly finished, heat a cast iron pan on the stove over high heat until smoking.

6. Remove the steaks from the bag and sear for 3 minutes per side, until a dark sear appears.

Nutritional Info: Calories: 1340, Sodium: 4308 mg, Dietary Fiber: 2.3 g, Total Fat: 116.5 g, Total Carbs: 26.3 g, Protein: 47.1 g.

Sous Vide Barbecue Beef Brisket

Servings: 12 | Prep time: 1 hour and 10 minutes | Cook time: 24-48 hours

Brisket can be cooked a number of different ways, but to get tender barbecue style brisket you need to let it cook for a long time. This recipe will show you how to use your Foodsaver and Anova to create authentic barbecue brisket in your home.

Ingredients:

1 (5-pound) beef brisket

4 tablespoons ground cumin

2 tablespoons smoked paprika

2 tablespoons dry mustard

3 tablespoons dark brown sugar

2 tablespoons ground rosemary

1 tablespoon cayenne pepper

3 tablespoons salt

1 cup your favorite barbecue sauce

2 teaspoons liquid smoke

Instructions:

1. Set your Anova to 137F/58.3C.

2. In a bowl, combine the cumin, paprika, mustard, sugar, rosemary, pepper, and salt.

3. Rub the spice blend all over the brisket and place in the refrigerator for one hour.

4. Remove the brisket from the refrigerator and coat, liberally, with half of the barbecue sauce.

5. Place the brisket in a vacuum-sealed bag and submerge in the water bath for 24 to 48 hours. Cooking for 24 hours will yield a firmer brisket, while 48 hours will produce flakier meat.

155

6. When the brisket is nearly finished cooking, heat your oven to 450F.

7. Remove the brisket from the water bath, coat with the remaining barbecue sauce and cook in the oven for 10 minutes.

8. Slice the brisket thinly against the grain and serve.

Nutritional Info: Calories: 414, Sodium: 2107 mg, Dietary Fiber: 1.4 g, Total Fat: 13.1 g, Total Carbs: 12.5 g, Protein: 58.4 g.

Sous Vide Korean Short Ribs

Servings: 6 | Prep time: 20 minutes | Cook time: 12 hours

Slow cooked short ribs become tender and flavorful because the connective tissue has a long time to break down. Cooking short ribs sous vide is the easiest, most fool proof way of achieving perfect texture.

Ingredients:

3 pounds short ribs

1/3 cup soy sauce

1/3 cup brown sugar

1/3 cup rice wine

1 tablespoon sesame oil

2 teaspoons black pepper

1/4 teaspoon cayenne

1 medium onion, peeled and quartered

8 garlic cloves, peeled

1 small Asian pear, shredded

1 (1-inch) chunk of ginger, peeled

2 teaspoons sesame seeds

Instructions:

1. Combine the soy sauce, brown sugar, rice wine, sesame oil, pepper, cayenne pepper, onion, garlic, pear, ginger, and sesame seeds in a large bowl.

2. Place the ribs in the bowl and refrigerate for 2 hours.

3. Set your Anova to 185F/85C.

4. Remove the ribs from the marinade and place directly into a vacuum-sealed bag.

5. Seal the bag and submerge in the water bath for 12 hours.

6. Remove the bag from the water bath and serve the short ribs over steamed rice.

Nutritional Info: Calories: 440, Sodium: 1048 mg, Dietary Fiber: 1.7 g, Total Fat: 10.9 g, Total Carbs: 22.7 g, Protein: 61.1 g.

Sous Vide Spicy Burger

Servings: 4 | Prep time: 30 minutes | Cook time: 50 minutes

This fresh take on the classic burger is packed with flavor and perfectly tender thanks to your Anova.

Ingredients:

2 pounds ground chuck

1 tablespoon vegetable oil

1 yellow onion, finely chopped

2 tablespoons minced fresh ginger

2 cloves garlic, finely chopped

2 teaspoons cayenne pepper

1 teaspoon ground cumin

1 teaspoon garam masala

2 teaspoons salt

4 sliced pepper jack or cheddar cheese

4 kaiser rolls

Instructions:

1. Set your Anova to 135F/57.2C.

2. Heat the oil in a saucepan over medium heat, and cook the onions, ginger, and garlic until soft.

3. In a large bowl, combine the beef with the onion mixture and cayenne pepper, cumin, garam masala, and salt. Mix well and form into 4 patties.

4. Place the patties in a vacuum-sealed bag and submerge in the water bath for 45 minutes.

5. When the burgers are nearly finished cooking, heat a cast iron pan over high heat. Remove the burgers from the bag, place in the pan, and top with a slice of cheese. Cook for 5 minutes or until the cheese begins to melt. Serve with the kaiser rolls.

Nutritional Info: Calories: 467, Sodium: 1699 mg, Dietary Fiber: 2.6 g, Total Fat: 23.8 g, Total Carbs: 36.1 g, Protein: 26.5 g.

Sous Vide Hanger Steak

Servings: 2 | Prep time: 15 minutes | Cook time: 1 hour

Hanger steak is just beginning to become popular thanks to its unique strong flavor. This recipe will show you how to make perfectly cooked hanger steak with a robust jus.

Ingredients:

1 pound hanger steak

2 tablespoons salt

2 tablespoons black pepper

3 tablespoons butter

1/2 cup low sodium chicken stock

1/2 cup red wine

1 sprig thyme

Instructions:

1. Set your Anova to 135F/57.2C.

2. Rub the hanger steak all over with salt and pepper and place in a vacuum-sealed bag with 1 tablespoon of butter.

3. Seal the bag and place in the water bath for 45 minutes.

4. While the steak is cooking, heat a pan on medium heat and add the chicken stock, wine, and thyme. Reduce by about half.

5. When the steak is finished, remove it from the bag and pour the liquid from the bag into the saucepan.

6. Heat a large cast iron pan over high heat and when smoking, add the steak, searing on all sides. Remove from the pan.

7. Slice the steak against the grain and drizzle with the jus to serve.

Nutritional Info: Calories: 677, Sodium: 7225 mg, Dietary Fiber: 2.3 g, Total Fat: 28.9 g, Total Carbs: 7.0 g, Protein: 83.5 g.

Sous Vide Beef Ribs

Servings: 6 | Prep time: 15 minutes | Cook time: 48 hours

Beef ribs are best cooked low and slow for tender fall off the bone meat. That can make cooking beef ribs at home a challenge, but thanks to your Anova it's just a matter of time.

Ingredients:

2 racks beef ribs

4 tablespoons salt

3 tablespoons black pepper

2 tablespoons dark brown sugar

2 teaspoons cayenne pepper

Instructions:

1. Set your Anova to 135F/57.2C.

2. In a small bowl, combine the salt, pepper, sugar, and cayenne.

3. Rub the spice mixture on the ribs, coating entirely.

4. Place the ribs in a vacuum-sealed bag and submerge in the water bath for 48 hours.

5. When the ribs are nearly finished, heat your oven to 500F.

6. Remove the ribs from the bag, place on a baking sheet and cook in the oven for 10-15 minutes to achieve a nice dark crust. Serve with your favorite barbecue sauce.

Nutritional Info: Calories: 74, Sodium: 3765 mg, Dietary Fiber: 1.0 g, Total Fat: 2.0 g, Total Carbs: 5.3 g, Protein: 9.0 g.

Sous Vide Beef Stew

Servings: 8 | Prep time: 30 minutes | Cook time: 6 hours

Beef stew is a hearty winter treat that can be stored very easily in the freezer thanks to your Foodsaver. This recipe will show you how to get the absolute best results by using your Anova rather than a slow cooker.

Ingredients:

1 cup thick cut bacon, cut into chunks

2 tablespoons butter

2 pounds sirloin or chuck roast, cut into chunks

2 carrots, cut into chunks

1 yellow onion, diced

2 cups red wine

2 cups low sodium beef stock

1 tablespoon tomato paste

1 clove garlic, chopped

1 sprig fresh thyme

1 bay leaf

Instructions:

1. Set your Anova to 140F/60C.
2. Heat a large skillet over medium heat and cook the bacon until fat is mostly rendered. Remove the bacon from the pan and add the beef, browning on all sides.
3. Add the carrots and onions to the pan and cook for about 10 minutes or until the vegetables start to soften.
4. Add the wine, stock, garlic, tomato paste, and thyme to the pan and bring to a boil.
5. Remove the pan from the heat and pour into a large vacuum-sealed bag.
6. Submerge the bag in the water bath and cook for 6 hours.

7.   Remove the bag from the water bath and serve. Leftovers can be resealed in a vacuum-sealed bag and frozen for later.

Nutritional Info: Calories: 457, Sodium: 957 mg, Dietary Fiber: 1.0 g, Total Fat: 21.9 g, Total Carbs: 5.7 g, Protein: 46 g.

Sous Vide Classic New York Strip Steak

Servings: 2 | Prep time: 10 minutes | Cook time: 45 minutes

The industry standard New York Strip has been a favorite of steak connoisseurs the world over and many steak houses have long relied on sous vide cooking to make sure every steak that leaves the kitchen is the perfect temperature. And honestly, there is no method better than sous vide to accomplish this.

Ingredients:

2 (12-16 ounces) New York Strip steaks

Salt and black pepper

2 tablespoons butter

1 tablespoon vegetable oil

Instructions:

1. Set your Anova to 125F/51.6C for medium rare or 130F/54.4 for medium.

2. Pat the steaks dry with paper towels and season liberally with salt and pepper. Place the steaks on a wire rack and leave, uncovered, in the refrigerator for one hour. They should appear dry.

3. Place the steaks in individual vacuum-sealed bags and submerge in the water bath for 45 minutes. They can be kept in the bath longer, but not longer than 3 hours. After that point the texture will be affected.

4. When the steaks are nearly finished, heat a cast iron pan on high heat with the oil until it is smoking.

5. Remove the steaks from the bag and sear for 3 to 4 minutes on each side, adding the butter midway through.

6. Remove the steaks from the pan and serve with a baked potato or creamed spinach.

Note: This recipe can also be used to cook ribeye, T-bone or Porterhouse steaks.

Nutritional Info: Calories: 840, Sodium: 235 mg, Dietary Fiber: 0 g, Total Fat: 35.4 g, Total Carbs: 0.4 g, Protein: 123.1 g.

Sous Vide Barbecue Tri Tip

Servings: 6-8 | Prep time: 15 minutes | Cook time: 6 hours

Tri tip is an excellent cut of beef that is just beginning to become popular so it can be tricky to figure out exactly how to cook it. This recipe will show you how to make perfectly juicy medium rare tri tip in your sous vide.

Ingredients:

1 (2-3 pounds) tri tip steak

1 tablespoon salt

1 tablespoon black pepper

2 teaspoons chili powder

2 teaspoons ground mustard

1/2 cup barbecue sauce

Instructions:

1. Set your Anova to 130F/54.4C.
2. Rub the tri tip with the salt, pepper, chili powder, and mustard.
3. Place in a vacuum-sealed bag and submerge in the water bath for 6 hours
4. When the tri tip is nearly finished in the water bath, heat your broiler to high.
5. Remove the tri tip from the bag and coat liberally with barbecue sauce. Broil for about 10 minutes or until the barbecue sauce begins to form a light crust. For a thicker crust, repeat this step with additional barbecue sauce.
6. Remove from broiler and slice against the grain to serve.

Nutritional Info: Calories: 370, Sodium: 1130 mg, Dietary Fiber: 0.6 g, Total Fat: 8.9 g, Total Carbs: 6.8 g, Protein: 61.8 g

Sous Vide Pulled Beef

Servings: 4 | Prep time: 30 minutes | Cook time: 24 hours

This barbecue favorite gets its fall-off-the-bone tenderness from a long low cook, and the unique blend of spices makes it really come alive.

Ingredients:

2 pounds beef brisket

4 sprigs of thyme

1 tablespoon olive oil

2 cloves garlic, smashed

1 bay leaf

1 yellow onion, chopped

1 large ancho chili, seeded and split

1 tablespoon tomato paste

1 tablespoon salt

1/4 cup your favorite barbecue sauce

4 kaiser rolls or hamburger buns

Instructions:

1. Set your Anova to 185F/85C.

2. In a large cast iron pan, heat the oil over medium-high heat and sear the brisket on all sides.

3. In a vacuum-sealed bag, combine the beef, thyme, garlic, bay leaf, onion, chili, tomato paste, and salt. Seal and submerge in the water bath for 24 hours.

4. Remove the bag from the water bath and remove the beef from the bag, discarding all other ingredients. Place the beef in a large bowl and shred with forks.

5. Serve on the rolls with a generous spoonful of barbecue sauce.

Nutritional Info: Calories: 675, Sodium: 2407 mg, Dietary Fiber: 3.9 g, Total Fat: 20.7 g, Total Carbs: 42.8 g, Protein: 75.6 g.

Sous Vide Beef Gyros

Servings: 4 | Prep time: 15 minutes | Cook time: 2 hours

This greek inspired wrap is simple but delicious thanks to perfectly cooked beef and just the right amount of seasoning.

Ingredients:

1 pound sirloin steak

2 tablespoons olive oil

2 tablespoons yogurt

1 cucumber, sliced

2 tablespoons lemon juice

2 tablespoons salt

2 tablespoons black pepper

4 large pita breads

Instructions:

1. Set your Anova to 130F/54C.

2. Rub the beef with the salt and pepper and place in a vacuum-sealed bag with the olive oil. Seal the bag and place in the water bath for 3 hours.

3. While the beef is cooking, combine the yogurt, cucumber, and lemon juice.

4. When the beef is finished cooking, remove from the bag and slice against the grain.

5. Place 1/4 of the beef on each pita bread and top with the yogurt sauce. Wrap and serve immediately.

Nutritional Info: Calories: 462, Sodium: 3894 mg, Dietary Fiber: 2.6 g, Total Fat: 15.1 g, Total Carbs: 38.9 g, Protein: 41.2 g.

15

DESSERTS

Sous Vide Dulce de Leche

Servings: 12 | Prep time: 5 minutes | Cook time: 12 hours

This topping can be difficult to make because it relies heavily on getting the temperature just right. Luckily, your Anova takes all of the guess work out of it by maintaining a perfectly consistent temperature at all times. Use this recipe as a topping for ice cream, cake or any dessert really.

Ingredients:

1 can sweetened condensed milk

Instructions:

1. Set your Anova to 185F/85C.
2. Pour the condensed milk into a vacuum-sealed bag and submerge for 12 hours.
3. Remove the bag from the water bath and immediately submerge in an ice water bath for 30 minutes. It can be used immediately, or stored in the refrigerator for later.

Nutritional Info: Calories: 80, Sodium: 32 mg, Dietary Fiber: 0 g, Total Fat: 2.2 g, Total Carbs: 13.6 g, Protein: 2.0 g.

Sous Vide Vanilla Poached Pears

Servings: 2 | Prep time: 10 minutes | Cook time: 1 hour

This healthy dessert recipe is easy to make and packs complex flavor as it cooks.

Ingredients:

2 pears, halved and cored

1 lemon, halved

2 tablespoons unsalted butter

2 tablespoons sugar

1 teaspoon vanilla paste or extract

Instructions:

1. Set your Anova to 185F/85C.

2. Mix the butter, sugar, and vanilla, and add to a vacuum-sealed bag. Add the pear halves and seal the bag.

3. Submerge the bag in the water bath and cook for 1 hour.

4. Remove the bag from the water and remove the pears. Slice the pears and drizzle the liquid from the bag over them to serve.

Nutritional Info: Calories: 282, Sodium: 85 mg, Dietary Fiber: 7.3 g, Total Fat: 11.9 g, Total Carbs: 46.8 g, Protein: 1.2 g.

Sous Vide Caramel Apple Rice Pudding

Servings: 6 | Prep time: 30 minutes | Cook time: 45 minutes

This rice pudding is enhanced with a rich caramel apple reduction that will delight your guests, and is sure to be perfectly cooked.

Ingredients:

2 tablespoons butter

2 apples, diced

1 cup arborio rice

1 teaspoon cinnamon

1/2 teaspoon ground ginger

1/4 teaspoon salt

1 1/2 cups cream

1 cup milk

1/2 cup caramel syrup

Instructions:

1. Set your Anova to 183F/84C.

2. In a large bowl, mix together the butter, apples, rice, cinnamon, ginger, salt, cream, milk, and caramel syrup.

3. Pour the mixture into a vacuum-sealed bag and submerge in the water bath for 45 minutes.

4. When the pudding is finished cooking, pour into a bowl and fluff with a fork before dividing among smaller bowls. The pudding can be served warm, or chilled in the refrigerator.

Nutritional Info: Calories: 250, Sodium: 167 mg, Dietary Fiber: 2.6 g, Total Fat: 8.3 g, Total Carbs: 40.3 g, Protein: 4.1 g.

Sous Vide Zabaglione

Servings: 4 | Prep time: 20 minutes | Cook time: 30 minutes

This Italian treat is so much more than a custard. Cooking in your Anova will bring out all of the subtle flavors for a satisfying dessert without a lot of work.

Ingredients:

4 egg yolks

1/2 cup champagne or other sparkling white wine

1/2 cup heavy whipping cream

1/2 powdered sugar

Instructions:

1. Set your Anova to 165F/74C.
2. Beat the eggs and add the sugar. Mix until the eggs have thickened and then add the champagne.
3. Pour the mixture into a vacuum-sealed bag and submerge in the water bath for 20 minutes.
4. While the mixture cooks, whip the heavy cream until stiff.
5. Remove the mixture from the water bath and pour into a large bowl. Refrigerate until the mixture is cool.
6. Remove the bowl from the refrigerator and fold in the whipped cream. Serve immediately.

Nutritional Info: Calories: 603, Sodium: 15 mg, Dietary Fiber: 0 g, Total Fat: 10.2 g, Total Carbs: 125.7 g, Protein: 3.0 g.

Sous Vide Rich Chocolate Mousse

Servings: 6 | Prep time: 30 minutes | Cook time: 30 minutes

This classic mousse is rich and decadent but not difficult to make. Impress your guest or yourself with the perfect results and delicious flavor of this perennial favorite.

Ingredients:

8 egg yolks

1 cup sugar

1/4 teaspoon salt

1/2 cup dry marsala wine

1/3 cup unsweetened cocoa

1/4 cup heavy whipping cream

Instructions:

1. Set your Anova to 165F/74.4C.

2. In a large bowl mix together the egg yolks, sugar, salt, and marsala wine.

3. Stir in the cocoa powder and heavy cream and mix until well blended.

4. Pour the mixture into a vacuum-sealed bag and submerge in the water bath for 15 minutes.

5. Remove from the water bath and massage the mixture to make sure it remains evenly mixed. Replace the bag in the water bath and cook an additional 15 minutes.

6. Remove the bag from the water bath and spoon the mousse into individual bowls. Serve warm or refrigerate for a cold mousse.

Nutritional Info: Calories: 242, Sodium: 111 mg, Dietary Fiber: 1.6 g, Total Fat: 8.5 g, Total Carbs: 37.4 g, Protein: 4.6 g.

Sous Vide Cinnamon Custard

Servings: 4 | Prep time: 20 minutes | Cook time: 1 hour

This light custard is enhanced with a touch of cinnamon. Your Anova will ensure that the consistency of the custard comes out perfectly.

Ingredients:

3 egg yolks

1/2 cup whole milk

1/2 cup cream

4 tablespoons sugar

1/4 teaspoon vanilla extract

1/4 teaspoon cinnamon

5 graham crackers (optional for topping)

Instructions:

1. Set your Anova to 185F/85C.

2. In a medium bowl, combine the egg yolks, milk, cream, sugar, vanilla, and cinnamon. Blend well.

3. Pour the mixture into a vacuum-sealed bag.

4. Submerge the bag in the water bath for 1 hour.

5. Remove from the water bath and serve. A simple topping for the custard can be made by pulsing 5 graham crackers in a food processor several times.

Nutritional Info: Calories: 198, Sodium: 134 mg, Dietary Fiber: 0.6 g, Total Fat: 7.8 g, Total Carbs: 28.4 g, Protein: 4.5 g.

Sous Vide Lemon Cheesecake

Servings: 6 | Prep time: 30 minutes | Cook time: 90 minutes

Cheesecake is one of the most decadent desserts out there, and it can be made easily in your Anova. This recipe introduces a hint of lemon to give your cheesecake a fresh finish.

Ingredients for crust:

1/2 teaspoon butter for greasing the ramekins

1/4 cup crushed graham crackers

2 tablespoons melted butter

1/2 tablespoon sugar

Ingredients for filing:

12 ounces cream cheese

1/2 cup sugar

1/4 cup sour cream

2 eggs

Zest of one lemon, chopped

2 tablespoons lemon juice

Instructions:

1. Set your Anova to 176F/80C.
2. Grease the ramekins with butter.
3. In a bowl, combine all of the crust ingredients and mix well.
4. Spoon equal amounts of the crust into each ramekin and press it to the bottom.
5. In another bowl, mix together the filing ingredients using a stand mixer or hand mixer.

6. Pour the filing evenly into the ramekins.

7. Place the ramekins side by side in a vacuum-sealed bag and make sure to keep it level. Seal the bag and place in the water bath for 90 minutes.

8. Remove the bag from the water and remove the ramekins from the bag. Let the cakes cool at room temperature for 1 hour and then cool further in the refrigerator. Serve chilled.

Nutritional Info: Calories: 361, Sodium: 245 mg, Dietary Fiber: 0 g, Total Fat: 27.8 g, Total Carbs: 23.4 g, Protein: 6.9 g.

Sous Vide Crème Brulee

Servings: 4 | Prep time: 30 minutes | Cook time: 2 hours

Crème Brulee is an elegant dessert that can be made in your Anova with very little work. They can be served plain or topped with seasonal berries.

Ingredients:

2 cups heavy whipping cream

4 egg yolks

1/4 teaspoon salt

1/3 cup sugar

Instructions:

1. Set your Anova to 190F/87.8C.
2. In a small pot, bring the heavy cream to a light boil and remove from heat.
3. Beat the eggs, and slowly add the sugar and salt. Add the cream and mix well.
4. Pour the mixture evenly into 4 ramekins and place ramekins inside a vacuum-sealed bag.
5. Seal the bag and place flat at the bottom of the water bath. Cook for 90 minutes.
6. Remove from the water bath and allow to cool overnight in the refrigerator.
7. Remove from the refrigerator and sprinkle each ramekin with a light coating of sugar.
8. Heat your broiler to high and cook until the top has caramelized. Or use a blow torch to caramelize the sugar. Serve warm.

Nutritional Info: Calories: 375, Sodium: 253 mg, Dietary Fiber: 3.8 g, Total Fat: 12.4 g, Total Carbs: 60.4 g, Protein: 6.2 g.

Sous Vide Poached Peaches

Servings: 4 | Prep time: 10 minutes | Cook time: 30 minutes

A healthy alternative to peach pie, this poached peach recipe will highlight the sweet and delicate flavor of any type of peach.

Ingredients:

2 peaches, halved

1 tablespoon dried lavender

1/4 cup water

1/4 cup honey

1/4 teaspoon salt

Instructions:

1. Set your Anova to 185F/85C.
2. Place the peaches in a vacuum-sealed bag and pour in the water, honey, lavender, and salt.
3. Seal the bag and submerge in the water bath for 20 minutes.
4. Remove the bag from the water bath and place in the refrigerator for 1 hour.
5. To serve, place one half peach in each bowl and top with the thickened cooking liquid.

Nutritional Info: Calories: 84, Sodium: 149 mg, Dietary Fiber: 0.8 g, Total Fat: 0.1 g, Total Carbs: 22.1 g, Protein: 0.5 g.

Sous Vide Blueberry Lemon Compote

Servings: 6 | Prep time: 10 minutes | Cook time: 2 hours

This compote can be eaten as on its own as a healthy dessert or used as a topping for pound cakes or cheesecakes.

Ingredients:

2 cups fresh blueberries

1/2 cup sugar

Zest of 1 lemon

2 tablespoons lemon juice

1 tablespoon butter

Instructions:

1. Set your Anova to 185F/85C.

2. In a large bowl, combine the blueberries, sugar, lemon zest and juice, and butter. Mix well.

3. Pour into a vacuum-sealed bag and submerge in the water bath for 2 hours.

4. Remove the bag from the water bath and pour into a bowl. Stir and either use warm or refrigerate for later use.

Nutritional Info: Calories: 111, Sodium: 15 mg, Dietary Fiber: 1.5 g, Total Fat: 2.2 g, Total Carbs: 24.7 g, Protein: 0.5 g.

Sous Vide Key Lime Custard with Graham Cracker Crumble

Servings: 6 | Prep time: 30 minutes | Cook time: 30 minutes

This deconstructed key lime pie is easy to make with your Anova, and healthier than a traditional pie.

Ingredients:

4 egg yolks

4 ounces key lime juice

1 can sweetened condensed milk

2 tablespoons brown sugar

6 graham crackers

2 tablespoons butter, melted

Instructions:

1. Set your Anova to 180F/82C.

2. In a large bowl, combine the lime juice, condensed milk, and egg yolks.

3. Pour the mixture into a vacuum-sealed bag and submerge in the water bath for 30 minutes.

4. While the custard cooks, place the graham crackers in a food processor with the brown sugar and butter. Pulse until combined.

5. Remove the custard from the water bath and place in the refrigerator until cool.

6. To serve, spoon the custard into individual bowls and top with the graham cracker crumble.

Nutritional Info: Calories: 306, Sodium: 182 mg, Dietary Fiber: 0 g, Total Fat: 12.6 g, Total Carbs: 42.9 g, Protein: 6.8 g.

Sous Vide Toffee Pudding

Servings: 6 | Prep time: 20 minutes | Cook time: 3 hours

This traditional English favorite can require time and skill to perfect, but your Anova will turn you into a master on your first attempt.

Ingredients:

5 tablespoons butter

1 teaspoon baking soda

1 teaspoon baking powder

1 cup hot water

1/2 cup light brown sugar

2 eggs, beaten

1 1/4 cups flour

Instructions:

1. Set your Anova to 195F/91C.
2. Grease 6 ramekins with a tablespoon of butter.
3. In a food processor, cream the butter until fluffy, add the eggs one at a time, then add the flour and baking powder.
4. Stir in the hot water and baking soda, and mix well.
5. Divide the mixture evenly between the ramekins and place them flat in a vacuum-sealed bag.
6. Seal the bag and submerge flat on the bottom of the water bath for 3 hours.
7. When the puddings are finished, remove from the water bath and carefully remove each pudding from its ramekin. Serve warm or refrigerate and serve later.

Nutritional Info: Calories: 247, Sodium: 305 mg, Dietary Fiber: 0.7 g, Total Fat: 11.3 g, Total Carbs: 32.2 g, Protein: 4.7 g.

16

Bonus:
Rubs and Seasonings
for Sous-Vide Masterpieces

The Ultimate Rub For Ribs, Pulled Pork, or Steaks

This is a great traditional rub that can be used for either pork shoulder, ribs or even steaks. Simply mix the ingredients and rub liberally all over the meat before vacuum sealing.

Ingredients:

1/2 cup paprika

1/3 cup dark brown sugar

1/4 cup kosher salt

2 tablespoons granulated garlic

1 tablespoon celery salt

1 tablespoon chili powder

1 tablespoon freshly ground black pepper

2 teaspoons onion powder

2 teaspoons dried thyme

2 teaspoons dried oregano

2 teaspoons mustard powder

1 teaspoon celery seed

1/2 teaspoon cayenne pepper

Instructions:

1. Combine all ingredients and rub liberally on the meat.
2. For the most robust flavor, apply rub and refrigerate for 2 hours before cooking.

Herbed Oil Marinade for Fish and Chicken

The olive oil will make either chicken or fish more tender, and a simple blend of aromatic herbs will lock in excellent flavor.

Ingredients:

1/2 cup extra virgin olive oil.

1 tablespoon fresh chopped rosemary

1 tablespoon fresh chopped thyme

1 teaspoon fresh chopped oregano

1/2 teaspoon chopped garlic

1 teaspoon kosher salt

1/2 teaspoon ground black pepper

1 tablespoon dry white wine

2 teaspoons whole grain mustard

Instructions:

1.   Combine all ingredients and use to marinate fish or chicken.

2.   For best results, do not marinade for longer than 3 hours before cooking.

Smokey Pepper Marinade for Steaks and Chops

Get that smoky grilled flavor with steaks and chops and a peppery kick that will make the meat really come alive.

Ingredients:

1/2 cup water

1/2 cup beer

3 tablespoons ground black pepper

2 teaspoons cayenne pepper

1 teaspoon ground mustard

1 tablespoon chopped garlic

1 tablespoon kosher salt

1 teaspoon liquid smoke

Instructions:

1. Combine all ingredients and use to marinade meat for at least 1 hour, but not more than 3 hours before cooking.

Hollandaise Held at The Perfect Temperature

Ingredients:

1 tablespoon lemon juice

1 stick (8 tablespoons) butter

3 egg yolks

1/2 teaspoon salt

Instructions:

1. Set your Anova to 149F/65C.

2. Combine all ingredients and mix well. Place in a vacuum-sealed bag and submerge in the water bath for 45 minutes.

3. Remove from the water bath and pour in a blender. Mix until smooth. The sauce can be served immediately, or poured back into the vacuum-sealed bag and held in the water bath for up to 3 hours.

Next Steps...

DID YOU ENJOY THE BOOK?

IF SO, THEN LET ME KNOW BY LEAVING A REVIEW ON AMAZON! Reviews are the lifeblood of independent authors. I would appreciate even a few words and rating if that's all you have time for. Here's the link:

http://www.healthyhappyfoodie.org/r2-freebooks

IF YOU DID NOT LIKE THIS BOOK, THEN PLEASE TELL ME! Email me at feedback@HHFpress.com and let me know what you didn't like! Perhaps I can change it. In today's world a book doesn't have to be stagnant, it can improve with time and feedback from readers like you. You can impact this book, and I welcome your feedback. Help make this book better for everyone!

About the Author

Isabelle Dauphin is a private chef extraordinaire who has prepared meals, specialty foods and beverages for celebrities along California's coast. With a background in nutrition, her highly creative yet nutritious recipes have won her a devout following and exclusive clientele. When she's not writing books, she spends her time developing new recipes and cooking up fresh servings of health and happiness for her clients and her family.

DO YOU LIKE FREE BOOKS?

Every month we release a new book, and we offer it to our current readers first...absolutely free! This helps us get early feedback before launching a book, and lets you stock your shelf full of interesting and valuable books for free!

Some recent titles include:

- The Complete Vegetable Spiralizer Cookbook
- My Lodge Cast Iron Skillet Cookbook
- 101 The New Crepes Cookbook

To receive this month's free book, just go to

http://www.healthyhappyfoodie.org/r2-freebooks